I'M NOT YOUR SUPERWOMAN

Whitney L. Brooks, *Visionary Author*

Co-Authored By:
Majeeda Bey, Pamela Branch, Felicia Goodman, Joanne Johnson, Andrea Joie', Ursula Jones, Lorna Kelley, Kisha Lesane, Tynesha Marie, Dr. Tabatha Spurlock, Shania Taylor, Marcella Tazewell

Copyright © 2022 by Empower Her Publishing, LLC
All Rights Reserved. This book, nor any portion thereof, may not be reproduced or used in any manner whatsoever without the expressed written permission of the publisher except for the use of brief quotations in a book review.

Printed in the United States of America.

ISBN: 979-8-83-544747-3
Edited, Formatted and Published by Empower Her Publishing, LLC

Table of Contents

Introduction v
Foreword by *Whitney L. Brooks* vii
My Values Matter More than My Circumstances
by *Majeeda Bey* 1
Wearing a Crown through a Crisis
by *Pamela Branch* 9
Know When to Take Me Time
by *Felicia Goodman* 13
I'm Not Your Superwoman, But I Am a Super Woman
by *Joanne Johnson* 19
Mask Off by *Andrea Joié* 27
The Cape Was a Load On My Back
by *Ursula Jones* 37
Our Capes May Have Holes, But We Can Still Fly
by *Lorna Kelley* 41
My Journey to Learning I Am Not Your Superwoman
by *Kisha Lesane* 49
Choosing Me…Intentionally by *Tynesha Marie* 55
Bouncing Back from Life's Setbacks Like a B.O.S.S.
by *Dr. Tabatha Spurlock* 63
The Wearing of the Cape by *Shania Taylor* 73
No Longer Boxed In by *Marcella Tazewell* 79
Conclusion 87

Introduction

I think we can all agree that the WOMAN is UNDERRATED! Constantly being pulled in various directions, she often falls in the trap of self-sacrificial exhaustion. The people who depend on her have literally grown in expectation of her "YES" that they're offended by her "NO." Finally, she becomes fed up with saving everyone but herself.

This book was written by women who, just like you, have poured into the needs and wants of everyone around them. Sure, as a mom, a wife, an employee, a business owner, a church member, a daughter, sister, auntie and all of the many other roles we fulfill, we have responsibilities. However, the message in this book is not neglecting those roles and the people who depend on you; it's simply not neglecting yourself in the process. It's about learning how to say "NO" to others so that you can say "YES" to yourself first.

As cliché as it sounds, you can't pour from an empty cup. The women in this book remind you that life happens, and that's okay, but it's your duty to be mindful of when you should take time just for you. Take a moment and be reminded of the things you love to do - perhaps before the kids or even before the spouse. What are some goals or dreams you never checked off your list? Where is your happy place - the place that makes you feel relaxed and recharged? When was the last time you put your phone on Do Not Disturb so that you could just be, without interruptions?

It's time to hang up the cape. You can't be everything to everyone and nothing to yourself. After reading this book, it is our hope that you feel confident enough to take back your power and deliberately began prioritizing YOU. You deserve that.

Foreword
Whitney L. Brooks

I did it.

I had been suffering in silence since the passing of my grandmother in 2015. I had watched my mother be strong for my sisters and me our entire lives and I just knew this, if no other time, was the time for me to be strong for her. So on days when I couldn't and didn't want to lift my body and the depression that weighed me down out of the bed, I still did. For my mama. She needed me.

It was the same routine daily. Get up, shower, get dressed, head to mom's - grab my cape on the way out the door. When I arrived, I would have to give her the same pep talk I had just given myself to get out of the bed. She had no idea and I didn't want her to. For at least the first year, our days consisted of being out and about, short trips to the outlets for lunch and shopping, local dining, strategizing ways to grow our new homecare business, booking vacations, networking. My mom was convinced that staying busy and on the go was the best way to keep her distracted from her grief. After I'd spent the entire day and night with my mom, I'd return to my house close to 10 pm every night – if not later, shower, go to bed, cry myself to sleep. Repeat.

Though losing my grandmother was undoubtedly the toughest part to process of my grief, realistically I was grieving a culmination of things. I had returned to work one week after burying my grandmother and spending time in North Carolina sorting through her belongings with the family. The dynamics at my job had already changed tremendously during previous months leading up to my grandmother's death and had really taken a turn when I gave my boss the heads up that I was looking for a new job. While planning to resign at some point, my emotional overwhelm combined with an utter lack of consideration and respect from my boss led to me resigning earlier than planned. I had no idea that the day I returned to work would be the day I would never come back.

It didn't hit me until the morning after when I officially submitted my resignation letter that I no longer had a job and no game plan for income. Moreover, what was my future going to look like from here on out? From the time I was a little girl, I knew I wanted to be a lawyer. I went to undergrad with plans of transitioning to law school right after. However, after graduating a year early, I went to work part-time at this company and after applying for a full-time opening with plans to study for the LSAT for a year, my boss (who had been a mentor since I was in high school) expressed my potential and her desire for me to be her successor as CEO. Law school went out the window and I officially began "CEO Training." So now that I had foregone my law school plans and had resigned from the job where I was training to be the next CEO, what was I going to do with my life?

I was in a tough space, trying to process a lot on my own. I felt like I really didn't have anyone to talk to the way I needed to. Not to mention, a month after my grandmother's passing, I also dissolved a friendship of eleven years. Within a month's time, I had lost my grandmother, my job, my mentor and my best friend. So it wasn't being there for my mom that was difficult; that was the thing I wanted to do. It was trying to find peace within my own struggles while trying to help her through hers too. Lord knows I wanted to do everything I could to be there for her, especially because my sister had to work and my stepfather had been recently deployed. All she had was me.

All of this was enough for me to do it then. But I didn't.

I thought I could fight this battle on my own. I had come from strong women. I had seen them overcome tough battles. Surely I could win this one. I just needed time.

But then, there was the business. Months prior to me leaving my job, my mom mentioned starting a homecare agency. I told her I would help her with the paperwork but I had no interest in running a business with her – or anyone else. I was going to be the next CEO at my company and I wouldn't have time. After I resigned and questioned how I was going to pay my bills and why I hadn't received any callbacks, not even for jobs that I was overqualified for, she reminded me of "the business" we had sitting on paper.

I had seen my mom dedicate her all to any job she worked (most recently as a Home-Health Aide) and she had maintained several side hustles as well. I knew she was an entrepreneur at heart and would be the most trusted business partner in the world. Nevertheless, there was a lot of stress and anxiety that came with the unknown. I didn't know the first place to begin with launching and growing a homecare business and it was an overwhelming journey trying to figure it out.

As I continued down the road of processing my grief, I recognized I never had the time. As a 24-hour agency, the business always needed me. During that time, I was in the gym nearly five, sometimes six days a week. That had really become my therapy. In addition to working out, I was eating clean and was down fifty pounds. But there were times, during my therapy session, where I had to stop mid-jog on the treadmill because the business needed me. Someone had called out of work for the night or something. Not a moment went by when I was able to just be – in my own thoughts, in my own space, on my own time. I didn't own the business. The business owned me. And I wanted out. Especially because even in the midst of us being so busy at times, I still wasn't bringing home enough personal income to pay my bills. The overheard expenses were eating up pretty much every dime of our revenue. As a result, two years after leaving my job and being a full-time entrepreneur, my house was listed for foreclosure.

I really needed to do it then. But still, I didn't.

Instead, I decided to shift my mindset. Although this was enough to knock me down, I refused to be defeated. Thankfully, my family was in a position to help me recover my house and after that, I got really serious about changing the trajectory of my life. I was all in. Despite the exhaustion the business brought upon me, I knew that if I just hung in there long enough, I would see a major return on my investment of time and efforts. Finally, I did.

Life was progressing and I was in a good place until I rekindled an old flame with a man I had been in a ten-year relationship with – on and off. This time our reconnection brought forth a child. Sadly, I was reminded of all the reasons I said it couldn't work each time we had broken up in the past. This time, however, we had a child involved and I hated it. I hated that deep down inside I knew I wouldn't have this perfect family that I had always imagined and I knew that when we separated this time, that it actually would be the very last time and he wouldn't make it easy for me. And he didn't. Over the years he had grown so used to my "yes" that my "no" was unacceptable. My "no" challenged him. So I found myself on the opposing side of the courtroom from the man that I had literally given my everything to for more than ten years for a painfully gruesome year-long custody battle. This was the toughest battle I had ever had to fight. After each court appearance, I came home, took off my cape and mended the holes back together with my tears and prepared for the next battle. I had honestly reached my breaking point, but I knew I couldn't give up.

I promised myself that when it was all over, I was really going to do it.

Each morning I was counting down until bedtime so my son would go to sleep so I could cry in peace. I didn't want him to see my tears. I didn't want him to know I was broken. He depended on me and I couldn't let him down.

Moreover, the pandemic had arrived and I volunteered to watch my nephew during the day while my sister and brother-in-law went to work. My sister had just confirmed babysitting with a trusted referral, but I didn't feel comfortable with my nephew being with anyone besides family during this time considering this severity of COVID-19. My nephew was only one at the time, just eight months younger than my son.

After keeping him nearly all day for four to five days per week, I soon realized that I had bitten off more than I could chew. I was watching two toddlers all day while also trying to strategize ways to run and grow my businesses, because by this time, I had three. I was exhausted. I didn't know if I was coming or going. I was numb to everything around me. The level of pain and anguish that I was experiencing on the inside made my head and my heart hurt. The days were for taking care of the babies. The nights were for crying. That left no time to really implement any of these business strategies and I was frustrated and overwhelmed. Just taking care of babies would've been fine if I wasn't a single mom who was responsible for the bills. But the reality was, I was a single mom and a full-time business owner, so if I didn't work my businesses, my businesses wouldn't work for me and I would never grow to the place I really wanted to be. I had been depressed before and never said a word. I would always just go about my day and manage my problems on my own. But this time was different. I actually told people I was depressed. I really wanted someone to be there for me, but it was like they couldn't hear my cry for help. Sadly, I think everyone who knows me is so used to me always being strong that the moment I mentioned I was struggling, they just felt I would get past it.

But I couldn't. I was suffocating and I wanted someone to save me, but no one did. In fact, they gave me less air. Everyone still continued to ask me to do this or do that. Each time, I would take a huge gasp of air and say "yes," until finally, I had no more breaths to take. I was tapped out. That was when I realized I had to save myself. I had to say "no" and with each "no" came a little more air. I started to breathe again. I began to set boundaries. But I knew that this was only a starting point. I didn't just need to set boundaries. I needed to heal.

So I did it.

I finally booked an appointment with a therapist to navigate through these tough experiences I've endured. I realized that taking care of me should be my top priority. I can't take care of my son if I'm not well. I can't be all that my family needs from me if I'm not at my best. So I'm hanging up the cape. It's time for me to save myself.

Perhaps counseling isn't your preferred way of saving yourself and that's okay. Before deciding on therapy, the biggest help for me was shifting my perspective on putting myself first and what that really means to me. I had to undergo a journey of self-reflection to really come to terms with the fact that putting me first was not selfish. I was worthy of the utmost care. I needed ME to set boundaries because if I didn't, I failed myself. It's no one else's responsibility to take care of me. That's my sole responsibility. Sadly, it wasn't until I became a mother that I really began to take back my power. My "no" became extremely personal because now, it was even bigger than me. My sweet baby depended on me and if I wore myself down trying to please everyone around me, what would I have left for him? Beyond that, is when I realized too, that it had to be bigger than my son as well. My "no" literally had to be for me.

Here are some ways in which I still show up for others while taking care of myself:

#1 - Setting boundaries. This looks like letting those close to me know what time I'm available to start taking calls each morning which allows me to start the day on my own terms. It also includes being specific about days which are exclusively dedicated to me or my son and me and not for others.

#2 – Not responding right away. I've learned that when I do things on my own time, people also learn that I'm going to do things on my own time. My need to always respond to a request right away to people please was crippling. I don't mind helping, but it's going to be during a time that best suits me.

#3 – Maintaining open communication. Part of my struggle was trying to do everything on my own and waiting until my breaking point to communicate my overwhelm. Now, I openly voice when I'm bothered, feeling a lack of reciprocation, or any other emotion evoked by someone else. Healthy communication leads to resolve.

#4 – Not biting off more than I can chew. Always saying yes always had me overwhelmed. I had to evaluate my to-do list and compare which of the tasks benefited me and which of them actually only benefited others. I was swamped with others' to-do lists that by the time I got to mine, I had no energy left to get it done. This required some adjusting. Additionally, this also meant not taking on more clients than I could handle at one time or even clients I knew wouldn't be worth the headache. I firmly believe that what is for me is for me so there was no regret in saying "no" to clients I didn't feel were a good fit.

I challenge you to undergo a journey of self-reflection as well. You're worthy of the undivided attention and care you've been neglecting yourself. You, and those who depend on you, will thank you for becoming a healthier, happier you.

My Values Matter More than My Circumstances

Majeeda Bey

It culminated with an emotional and tearful conversation with my employer, where I finally acknowledged the truth I had been holding onto for months: I needed to resign. In that moment, I realized, or at least was willing to admit aloud, that I couldn't do it all. I couldn't keep all the balls in the air and operate at the standard I set for myself. I had been so used to wearing my (Superwoman) cape that just being "Clark Kent" felt like a disappointment. When you're so used to being strong and holding things together, appearing weak feels like defeat. Why, after 16 years in my career, would I be willing to just let it all go? It was simple: who I was becoming and who I desired to be no longer fit me staying in the same position. I wanted room to grow, blossom and create my own definition of success, and if there wasn't space for me to grow there, I needed time and space to create it elsewhere.

I'm no Superwoman. I'm human. I get tired, frustrated, overwhelmed, stressed, and anxious, while often suffering in silence, yet screaming for help on the inside. I'm the single mother, loyal friend, devoted daughter, sibling and dedicated employee who also NEEDS help, but rarely asks. I realized that I often found the time and energy to support and attempt to meet everyone else's needs and found little time to prioritize my own. One could even say that I didn't know what I wanted outside of what other people wanted for or from me. Who has time for "self-care" when you're balancing children, a job, a few businesses, practice schedules, family matters, and the everyday demands of life? I'll admit: I chose (or was chosen) to carry the torch and be the change I wanted to see for our family, so I couldn't just settle or accept life as it was. I had to seek new opportunities, find ways to grow and get better, improve my station in life, and truly thrive! I wanted more from life and I had to go get it!

Consequently, I rarely slowed down, stopped, evaluated or considered whether what I was doing or the direction I was going in was even what or where I truly wanted to be. The pandemic of 2020-2021 was my wakeup call. Over that time period, I had the opportunity to do something I hadn't done in a long while - be still. I had gotten so accustomed to the routine (rut) of life and being on the go, that I hadn't taken time to think of doing much else. When I was forced to pause and do things differently, I seriously asked myself, *'What are you doing? Why are you spinning your wheels, meeting other people's expectations, wearing WAY too many hats, yet don't even know what you're doing it for?'* I thought I did. I was being responsible. I was being supportive. I was making sacrifices. I was doing what I was *supposed* to do, right? Wrong. I had it all wrong. I was existing, not living. Yes, I was making a steady income and even had multiple streams of income, yet somehow, I seemed to be working just enough to catch everything up. Don't get me wrong. I want it all - travel, freedom, wealth, fulfillment, significance, purpose, connection, the full experience of life, but the way I was going about it just wasn't adding up.

My Values Matter More than My Circumstances

The Priority Has to Be You! There is little time to take care of you AFTER you take care of the house, the children, the significant other, the job, the bills, the future, the <u>fill in the blank</u>. I regularly made time for everything and everyone else, except me. From the time I woke up in the morning to the time I went to bed at night, I would spend the majority of my day reacting and responding to the demands of other people and things outside of me. I filled the roles of the maid, the chef, the facilitator, the admin, the hair stylist, the treasurer, the chauffeur, the employee, the boss, the mediator, the teacher, the comforter, the DJ (for sing-alongs in the car), the host, the producer, the financial coach, the friend, the daughter, the sister, the landlord, the property manager, the freelancer, the independent contractor, the MOM, the <u>fill in the blank</u> <u>and pick up the pieces</u>. I could show up daily for work, enroll my children in extracurricular activities for their enjoyment and well-being, manage a household, and pursue business endeavors, yet I didn't make consistent time in the course of any given day just for me.

I reached my late 30s before I became keenly aware that I was rarely, if ever, on my own schedule. I finally reached a crossroads that forced me to take inventory of where I was, how I got there, and consciously make the decision to STOP. I didn't feel like I could complete another task, pursue another goal, or add yet another thing to my never-ending to-do list without really taking inventory of what I was doing it all for. Once I understood that, then I could make the shift. I had gotten to where I didn't care about what I could accomplish because I didn't quite feel fulfilled from anything I was doing. I was simply going through the motions without much thought and I knew within that I needed to pivot.

As I sought for a solution, the phrase "the priority has to be you" reverberated through my mind. I often heard these words mentioned by someone I had grown to admire and respect and who modeled this philosophy. She promoted optimal health AND she not only talked the talk, she walked the walk. As a woman in her early 50s, she was physically fit, mentally tough, spiritually sound, and emotionally intelligent. Although we often hear about self-care, how often do we actually see it modeled in someone's everyday life? Needless to say, the idea of optimal health was extremely attractive. I didn't know what that truly meant or even looked like, but I knew I would continue to slip further into a constant state of anxiety, stress, and overwhelm if I didn't do something drastically different. I didn't just need to make a change, I needed to be transformed.

I initially decided to *just* participate in a 7-day fruit and veggie challenge as a means to shift my focus and help me physically feel better. I had completed this challenge once before and got great results, so I knew the benefits of "giving my body what it needed to thrive". The challenge started on February 1st, 2022. I set my initial first quarter business goal aside to just focus on prioritizing myself, or at least developing some minimal standards, as it related to my mind, body and spirit. Little did I know, I would be taking the first pivotal step toward creating a new identity and increasing my capacity to do even greater than I had previously done.

I completed the challenge and released nine pounds, felt more energized, and had better rest, but that was only the beginning. The coaching I had received encouraged me to keep going to get even greater results. There was an offer to participate in a 45-day Sugar Ain't Sweet program and although I didn't know fully what I was signing up for, I knew I was worth the investment. Since I was struggling with being on my schedule, I wanted - no needed - to KNOW what prioritizing me meant and felt like. How could I take on the challenge to go from not being on my schedule at all to actually prioritizing me first?

Over that 45-day period, I learned what that consistently looked like. Prioritizing me looked like starting and ending my day with me. Before the children arose, before I checked my phone, even before the sun came up, I gave myself time to think, exercise, read, pray, meditate, plan. At the end of the day, I could do the same. I learned to put aside the demands of my children and others to take time to myself. Sure, I often had to wake up earlier just to do so, but it was well worth it. Given that my body was in better shape, I actually had more energy from less rest and could easily wake up to give myself ME time. It meant making decisions that put me first instead of last. It meant making my health and well-being the big rock in the jar of my life, not the pebbles or the sand that get filtered in AFTER everything else - the job, the children, the household duties, etc. - had taken up all the space in the jar. Prioritizing me meant saying NO to others, even when I didn't necessarily want to, so that I could say yes to my priorities, my values and me.

Needless to say, that sacrifice of taking 45 days to put me first changed everything. It gave me a very clear perspective of how I could order my life for my sake and the sake of those who rely on and interact with me. Each day I continue to chase and remind myself of that version of me – how good I felt, how clear my mind was, how practical and achievable it was. That version of me knows what she wants. She knows and demands what she deserves. She knows what she's willing to sacrifice to get it. She prioritizes based on her values without apology, decides based on her objectives and stands firm on what she believes in. She recognizes that she doesn't need to be anyone's superwoman. She can just be a woman, and that is enough.

Majeeda Bey is a native of Richmond, VA and a Virginia Tech graduate from the Charles E. Via Jr. Department of Civil & Environmental Engineering program. Since graduating in 2006, she has enjoyed a successful 16-year career in project management with a concrete construction company and has developed into a leader within her firm and industry. Along with managing her full-time career, she is a devoted mother to two daughters who inspire her to continually grow and become better so they have an example to look up to and a model to follow. In addition to her job, Majeeda is also a licensed professional in the financial services industry, where she advocates for individuals and families to develop strong financial foundations and implement financial concepts to help move them toward financial independence. Most recently, she applied for and obtained a license as a commercial contractor in an effort to expand her capacity, provide more opportunities for growth and increase diversity within the construction industry. Her aim is to add value to others by personally developing and stretching herself to both maximize her potential and fulfill her unique purpose in life.

Keep in touch with Majeeda via the web:
www.BrownandBey.com
Facebook: Majeeda Bey
Instagram: @majeedabey

Acknowledgements

ShaQuantia Smith
Instagram: @the_z_show

Nancy Buchanan
Arbonne
Nancybuchanan.Arbonne.com

Shaaron Atkins-Comfort

Arabia El

Yasmeen A Bey
Yasmeenbey109@yahoo.com

Shani Kreager
Young Living Essential Oils
https://essentiallyspoiled.lifestepseo.com

Ada Ari
Ada Ari Books
www.ada-ari.com
Facebook: @AdaAri
Instagram: @Ada_ari

Tezrah El

Kenya Motley

Renee Adkins Jones
Friend Association For Children

Wearing a Crown through a Crisis
Pamela Branch

"A crown, if it hurts, is not worth wearing." – Pearl Bailey

Tuesday, September 30, 2003, was the day that my whole life changed. It started out as an upbeat, warm day full of possibilities. It was going home day from the hospital for my mom and I was there to pick her up. My mom had battled her weight for years and it had taken a toll on her knees. My mom had a successful bilateral knee surgery the day before, but the day quickly changed at mid-morning into a day that causes me panic attacks to this very day as I frequently replay the events that led up to mid-morning. That day, I was alone at my mother's bedside and watched her fall into respiratory distress as she attempted to work with the physical therapist. Her eyes were weary, her body was not cooperating, and her breathing was labored. As a medical professional, she knew that something was wrong, but she kept fighting until she couldn't any longer. Her eyes glazed over as she collapsed on the bed. I saw this regal, poised, and composed mother look scared and confused. The physical therapist hastily left the room, but never returned. I pressed the call button for help, but no one came. I ran down the hospital hallway and no one even recognized my desperation. I yelled for help and finally a nurse followed me to the room and then pushed me out. The staff worked to revive my mother for 40 minutes only to come out and say that they could not bring her back. That morning, my mother died from an unexpected pulmonary embolism. The woman who had raised me for 35 years to be the independent, driven, and compassionate person that I am was gone. I had to call my father and brother to tell them what had happened.

For 35 years, I saw her try to be perfect for my father, my brother and me, her friends, her church family, but not necessarily the best person she needed to be for her. The trauma of that day will never leave me. Each time my mother's birthday comes in July and each September, I have a private moment of panic that something tragic might be lurking around the corner again to turn my world upside down. On September 30th of each year, I think about how she was the queen in our family and whether she carried her crown with undeserved pressure until her last day.

Since 2003, I have tried to push away the pain of that day whenever I have a similarly traumatic or stressful event. I want to honor my commitment to be the poised and professional woman that my mother raised me to be. For the next year after my mother's passing, I was engrossed in planning what I hoped would be the perfect wedding and reception at my alma mater. At 36, I was getting married for the first time. After my mom's death, everyone I knew could appreciate a celebration to reverse the sadness, one where my mom's presence would be felt. My wedding director had everything in order, but I wanted to be involved in all the small details. I envisioned a beautiful, dazzling day, but it turned out to be a dark, cloudy day in August 2004 with torrential rain. Despite the rain, which I later learned was good luck, the day turned out to be all that I had hoped because I allowed trusted family and friends to help carry my load, support me in the pain of my mother's absence, and share in the joy of that day and the years since. When the final dance was done and I went to my room to relax, I collapsed on the floor of the hotel room. I cried because the flood of anxiety and panic I had bottled up during months of planning had to have somewhere to go and so it did. My mom was supposed to be there. One milestone down, more to come.

In April 2005, I learned that I was pregnant. I instantly thought about my mom who told me the year before she died that she was so looking forward to being a grandmother. As an older mom-to-be, my OB/GYN had advised of all the markers that are associated with having a baby later in life. My mother had me at age 23 after more than one miscarriage. I tried to push that possibility out of my mind. My doctor shared that my blood work indicated that there was a 75% possibility of Down's Syndrome or spina bifida. I sat in the doctor's office in disbelief, ridden with anxiety. I tried to fight back the tears of that possibility. I prayed all the way to work after my appointment and called my husband to tell him the results. He reassured me everything would be fine, but my mind kept racing back to the doctor's words. At that time, I was also representing children with special needs and listening to the distressed stories of parents whose children were marginalized by school administrators and ridiculed by their peers. On December 14, 2005, at 4:06 p.m., after only five hours of active labor, I had a beautiful daughter who was perfect in every way. I named her Jacquelyn after my mom. As someone who had wanted to be a mother for a while, the anxiety of being at home with a little person who would not let me sleep or eat was overwhelming. I experienced postpartum depression to the point that I would just sit and cry for hours the week before and after Christmas, longing for the time when I could get back to work.

Finally, after working 10 years for others with expectations that did not elevate or edify what I felt most vital to practicing law, I was again forced to make another life changing decision – whether to go into solo practice. In February 2016, I knew that a job that I had been excited to take on would have to come to an end. So, after four months of preparation, on June 20, 2016, I took the plunge and with support from my family, took a leap of faith into opening a solo practice where I would be able to focus on educating and representing clients who had experienced their own trauma in the workplace. It sounds strange for a lawyer to say this, but that's why we are called Attorneys and Counselors at Law. We argue and fight for our clients. We also do a fair amount of counseling with clients who encounter anxiety, stress and trauma due to microaggressions, denied opportunities, pay cuts, redundant and unappreciated efforts, demotions, terminations, and false accusations at work.

I will probably never understand why the events of September 30, 2003 occurred. However, the crown that my mom wore as she attempted to be the best wife, mother, and friend is not worth the pressure that we as Black women place on ourselves to be the modern superwoman. We are human, we need support, and we are allowed to fail. The people around us need to see that we can be both virtuous and vulnerable, and it's okay. There are days I am too exhausted to talk, cook dinner, take a call or attend a meeting. I love my crown, but I will not let wearing it hurt me.

Pamela Branch is a native of Richmond, Virginia. She has been a practicing attorney for 25 years and specializes in representing employees and persons who need a good advocate. Pamela graduated with a B.A in English/Women's Studies from Westhampton College at the University of Richmond. She received her Juris Doctor from the T.C. Williams School of Law at the University of Richmond. Pamela has been married for 17 years to her wonderful husband, H.T., and they have one daughter, Jackie.

Learn more about Pamela by visiting www.richmondlegalgroup.com.

Know When to Take Me Time
Felicia Goodman

When you think of the word Superwoman, what comes to mind? For me, it is a woman who can do it all. Doing it all, however, comes with a sacrifice and sometimes means doing without for the sake of others.

Growing up, my mom was the person who did everything around our home, as she was a stay-at-home housewife and my dad worked and was the financial provider. I looked at my mom as a super woman; there was nothing she couldn't fix around the house. Rarely did I see her take time for herself. Being a housewife was a full-time, twenty-four seven job. There was always something that needed to be done. She was always busy making sure we had clean clothes to wear, cooking the family meals, cleaning the house or just spending time with my brothers and me. I knew it couldn't have been easy raising four kids, having a husband and a household, but she made it look seamless. She was my blueprint for what a woman should do for her family and home to make sure everyone's needs were taken care of. So as I developed into a young lady, woman, mother and wife, I took on the same mentality.

Before becoming a wife, however, I was a single parent and I always wanted to make sure that my daughter was provided for. She deserved the best. In order to make that happen, I worked two jobs. One job was full-time and the other part-time and sometimes I worked during the holidays as seasonal help at one of the local department stores just to make sure my daughter had what she needed. It wasn't always easy but as a single parent I was willing to do what I had to do, whether it was a struggle or not. Trying to find a balance while juggling multiple jobs became extremely overwhelming, but I knew quitting was not an option because I had someone who was dependent on me and I didn't want to let her down. Due to my work schedules, there were times when I missed major milestones because I was working so many hours, but I tried to be there for my daughter as much as I could. At times I felt guilty about not being able to be at some of the events, but in my heart, I felt I was doing the right thing at that time and prayed she would understand. When I reflect on those times of not physically being present, those are times I can never get back. As a mother, I never want to disappoint my child and I felt torn between being able to provide by working or missing time to attend an event she had at school. There were days when I was extremely exhausted and didn't know how I was going to function from day-to-day but I kept pushing. The thought of taking a break or time out for myself was never an option, so I kept plunging forward each day.

When I got married, it all intensified. I had to make sure that the house was in order, bills were paid on time, the husband was taken care of and again, there was no personal time for myself. I reverted to my mom and remembered it is always left up to the woman to make sure that the house is clean, and if it wasn't, that was a reflection of me and my inability to keep a clean house. The blame is never placed on the male because he is classified as the financial support; it is the woman. The only difference between my mom and me was I had a full-time demanding job and a business that I was building on the side. There were days I would work 12-hour shifts but still had another five to six hours of things that needed to be done at home. I had to keep that superwoman cape on 24x7 just to make sure things stayed afloat, and if I took it off, things would surely fall apart - so I thought. I knew at the rate I was going I wouldn't last and that I would become depleted because I was burning both ends of the candle. I wasn't able to recharge nor had I learned how to say no or ask for help.

Many women feel that we should do it all. I surely fell into that mindset but the reality is, we can't, and sadly at times, pride will not allow us to ask for help. We will go to any lengths to get things done and we suffer because of the lack of taking personal time to recharge, so that we can become better versions of ourselves. I thought asking for help was a sign of weakness. I convinced myself that the woman is supposed to make sure that everyone is taken care of first and then she is last. I soon learned that lesson was not the case as I was always there for everyone else, but no one was there when I needed assistance. The few times I did ask for assistance or help, I would get responses like, "you should have called me earlier," or "I am busy right now," or "call me tomorrow around the same time and I should be free." When I was called, I didn't give excuses. I was there with no questions asked. It was during this time that I began to reflect on the things and people I was around and what the spectrum of our relationship entailed. Was it give and take or take and take? Once I realized that I was not valued in the same way, things began to change, especially for those I helped in the past. When a favor couldn't be reciprocated, I became less and less accessible - not intentionally, but I was busy or had things already scheduled that couldn't be changed. That is when I made up my mind that I would be putting myself first and if someone asked for assistance, I would lend a hand if I was available. If not, I would tell them no. The first time I said no, I must admit that I felt kind of bad for not being able to help them out or I just did not want to. Soon after, it became very empowering. I didn't say no to be mean, but it was my time to do what I wanted and not be at the beck and call of others.

In today's world, women are reclaiming their power, personal time, independence and concentrating on self-care, which is at the top of the list. There are so many women who are suffering in silence and more and more are recognizing that that shouldn't be the norm. It wasn't until after becoming severely burnt out and exhausted that I knew something had to give. I recall a time many years ago when I was just going and going and not stopping to even eat. My body wouldn't allow me to function and it shut me down for a few days because I needed to rest. After that, I really started taking time for myself. It was difficult to do at first because when you are used to continuously going and then suddenly you must come to a screeching halt, it makes you feel inadequate. Sadly, I wouldn't even take a minute because I would feel guilty like there were a million things that I should be doing. Once I realized that I was important too and it was okay to unplug and take a break from everything to recharge and reset, I started scheduling self-care appointments on the weekends and sometimes small breaks during the week would be dedicated to relaxation. I now have regular scheduled days of pampering that can be anything from a spa day, hair care and nail services or spending the day in the park with a good book, a bottle of wine and snacks. My most relaxing place is at the beach listening to the sound of the ocean waves. It puts me into a place of ultimate tranquility while also listening to smooth jazz. After I have recharged, I am a better person to those around me. I can think clearly and my mental state is in a better place. I still practice saying no to those things that are not in alignment with my energy along with not allowing people to make me feel bad because I don't have the time to assist them with their requests. Taking time for you is a must and I practice self-care more than I ever have in the past. Just like you put gas in your car on a regular basis, you need to recharge your mind, body and soul. Find the things you desire, get back in tune to those things that used to bring you joy and make it a regular practice to do it weekly if you can. If not, try bi-weekly. If those two don't work for your schedule, try to do it monthly, but take that time. It is necessary for you to be the best you mentally and physically. It's time to take back your power and put you first.

Felicia Goodman was born in Vicksburg, Mississippi. She is a funny, sometimes shy, but very compassionate and creative person. She is a mother of one daughter, a son-in-love and a new Mimi to a wonderful grandson born during the pandemic. She is a 30-year experienced Cosmetologist who enjoys crafting, home décor, music festivals, wine tasting and just relaxing on the beach. Her professional career has been in the medical field for the last 35 years working with a variety of physician specialties. She is also the owner of Diva Fashion Collections and Home Décor, which was birthed in May of 2011 due to her love for fashion and home decorating. Felicia has displayed her fashions at some of the biggest festivals over the years, to include the Tom Joyner Family Reunion in Orlando, Florida, Steve Harvey Hoodie Awards in Atlanta, Georgia, and the International Women's Conference in Baltimore, Maryland. She can now add co-author to her many accomplishments.

Stay connected with Felicia online by following her on Facebook and Instagram at Diva Fashion Collections & Home Décor.

Acknowledgements

Tammy Cleveland

Mikkea Copeland

Pamela Griffin-Armstead
Mary Kay
www.marykay.com/pgriffin-armstead
Facebook: Your Fabulous Skin
Instagram: @griffinarmstead

I'm Not Your Superwoman, but I Am A Super Woman

Joanne Johnson

Writing my story isn't easy because sharing instances of pain forces me to be emotionally vulnerable. I have wanted to tell my story for years and I believe now is the time. If sharing my truth can help a woman change her life, I know it will be worth it.

It has been necessary for me to relearn the power of saying no! It's easy to fall back into old habits especially as a person who loves helping others. I have always enjoyed being able to comfort people, to make their load lighter, and to be honest, it made me feel good about myself. Serving others filled a void in my life when I didn't feel needed.

Over the years, society has taught women to serve others, but for some, it goes deeper. For me, it all started as a child, always running around at the church eager to serve the seniors during potluck dinner. I loved going to get their food. The older people would be so happy and their smiles made me feel important. I didn't feel important at home because my dad was abusive to my sister and me. When my sister and I were about six and seven years old, he beat us badly then stomped on our dollhouses because we had been playing with baby powder and spilled it all over our bedroom floor. Then, another time when he was angry, he broke my sister's bridal doll head off. Sometimes we had to sit for hours rubbing his back because he was hurting. Due to our dad's abuse, both my sister and I ran away from home at a very early age. Runaways often find themselves in lots of compromising situations that wear them down. They lack the funds to provide for themselves, so they must learn to depend on others. My father didn't show love to me, so I started looking for it in the men I met. I used to think that if I had sex with a guy, he would love me. Eventually, I realized the men were using me for their own selfish pleasures. Due to my low self-esteem, I had a hard time feeling that I deserved better. All the bad things that happened and things people had said to me skewed my perception of who I really was. After suffering through and surviving rape several times and finding myself in abusive relationships, it began to beat me down mentally. The first time I was raped was by the Confederate Angels motorcycle gang. I was twelve years old and they had given me Vodka to drink when I asked for water.

After many failed relationships and two marriages, I started to see the wrong path that I had been following and was determined to change its course. I started to learn to love myself and realized that no matter what someone told me in the past, I was important. It took baby steps for me to learn how to change how I responded to relationships and take the time I needed to work on myself.

Eventually, I fell in love with a man who became my third husband. Our relationship was rocky for the first fourteen years because of his drinking problem, but he was supportive of my son and me. Traumatic events in our past had caused deep emotional pain for both of us and we were trying to find our way. Finally, in 2004, I gave my life to Christ, and soon after, he did too. I would love to tell you we had a perfect marriage after that, but no marriage is perfect. It still took several years after giving our lives to Christ before our relationship began to take a turn for the good. But I knew without a doubt he was the man that God intended for me.

The next eleven years were great and we both had changed so much. We took in his grandson and eventually adopted him. My life was finally on the right track and I was enjoying it. I had a husband who adored me! Suddenly, our life became torn apart when the doctors told us that he had an aggressive tumor in his bladder. We learned the inevitable truth: that my husband only had a short time to live. He died just two months after being diagnosed with cancer. I loved Ojay very much and seeing him deteriorate so quickly and suffer in pain was hard on us. My health issues made it hard to care for my husband but I had support from my church family who were with me from the beginning to the end.

After Ojay died, I didn't plan on getting involved in a relationship with anyone, but an ex-boyfriend found out my husband passed and began calling me. I had been very much in love at one time with this man and still cared about him. Over the years, both my husband and I were very close to many of his family members. I had broken up with him because after he had served in Vietnam, he had become heavily involved in drug use. I wasn't aware of his drug use when we started dating but after several years, I could no longer handle the ups and downs of life with an addict. He is clean now and was persistent that now was our time to get it right. My old fears resurfaced because I had always had a man in my life, good or bad, and I had never been alone. I began to question everything in my life but finally, we started dating again.

In the beginning, things were good between us and he helped distract me from dwelling on the loss of my husband. Things began going downhill quickly for us because when someone stops using drugs it doesn't mean mentally, they have changed. He still had the same mindset as before and I had forgotten how jealous he was in the past. My emotional health began deteriorating as I found myself entangled again in a spiraling down relationship. He constantly implied I was hiding someone when I didn't answer him on the phone or on Facetime right away. He would call back-to-back several times in a row and it started stressing me out. The constant accusations were keeping me stressed out and calls to my sister-in-law were overwhelming for her as well. Another issue in our relationship was him not respecting the boundaries that I had set for myself and this was unacceptable for me. It is important for me that in any relationship I am in that the other person respects my wishes. After I was very clear about certain things, he still wanted to do things his way and my silence allowed him to take me for granted. I was afraid that if I called the relationship quits that he would go back on drugs or that he wouldn't let the relationship go that easily. How had I allowed myself to end up in this situation again after working so hard to change? Wasn't I the one who always told other people: People treat you the way that you allow them to treat you?

At first, I felt like I was becoming weak again, but in fact, I was becoming stronger. I had finally had enough! I deserved better and was not going to allow anyone to make me afraid to be me. I realized that I couldn't stay in the relationship because I was afraid that he would return to drugs. It would be his own choice and not my responsibility if he decided to start using drugs again. We are now friends and thankfully, he is still drug-free.

I began to look at other areas of my life where I found it hard to say no. Some people always seemed to need help but didn't reciprocate or used tactics to manipulate me because I have a big heart.

The following areas were helpful for me to work on regaining control of my life.

1. I took a good look at myself to discover why I had a problem saying no.

2. I recognized the ways people used manipulation to get me to do what they wanted and I stopped letting them.

3. I prioritize my needs over others. It's in my DNA to help others and I believe that is what God intends for us to do. I will continue to help others and remain active in community outreach events. But just as in anything else, there needs to be moderation to take care of yourself to be able to give back to others.

My past does not define who I am and no matter what has happened in my life, I will not let it deter me from reaching my dreams. My goal is to use my life, my pain, and my gains to empower women to become agents of change, not only for themselves, but for their families and our community. No longer am I afraid to do this alone because I am not your Superwoman, but I am a Super Woman!

Joanne Johnson

Joanne Johnson is an entrepreneur, author, mother, and grandmother who resides in Richmond, Virginia. After years of defeating traumatic experiences of rape, domestic violence, and low self-esteem from an early age, she has learned how to use her pain to change her past into creating a better future, finding social support, and giving back to the community. Building strong relationships in her professional and personal life is the foundation for everything she does. Her professional accomplishments include an MBA, Member of the Gold Key International Honor Society, Assistant Correctional Chaplain, Certified Chronic Disease Self-Management Leader, and Lifestyle Consultant Specialist. Her volunteer experiences include working with the Community Emergency Response Team, Medical Reserves Corp, and the Red Cross Disaster Team.

Acknowledgements

Cathy Woodard
M&M Tax Consulting Firm LLC

Margo Shorter
Blessed Arts
www.blessedarts.net
Instagram: @Blessedarts1

Dennis Parker
Dr. Dennis
www.drdpinspires.com
Instagram: @drdennisparker

Claudia Massey
Certified Life Coach
WWW.CLAUDIAMASSEY.COM
Facebook: @coachclaudiamassey
Instagram: @coachclaudiamassey

Naomi Odero

Donna Denson
The Lashes
www.toribellecosmetics.com/?webalias=thelashes
Facebook: Donna Campen Denson
Instagram: @DonnaDenson2

Paul Tashner
Car CastleRVA
www.CarCastleRVA.com
Facebook: Car Castle
Instagram: @carcastle
LinkedIn: @carcastlerva1

Celestine Harvey
PHAT MAMMAS KITCHEN LLC
Facebook: @phatmammaskitchen or Celestine Harvey
Instagram: @Phatmammas_kitchen

Wendy Jansen
Bankers Life
Bankerslife.com
Facebook: Wendy Ferrara Jansen
Instagram: Wendy Ferrara Jansen
LinkedIn.com/wendyferrarajansen

Gwen Mills
Gwen's Studio Paparazzi Jewelry
www.gwenmillsstudios.com
Facebook: Gwen Mills Studios
Instagram: Gwen Mills Studios

Mask Off
Andrea Joié

"You're strong. You've got this." Really, I didn't have it. I didn't even know what "it" was. I could barely look at myself in the mirror from disgust or pick myself up out of the bed on a day-to-day. I knew I did not have it. At the time, so many didn't understand how weak I was. I needed help. I needed understanding. I needed counseling.

"Inherent in labeling someone "strong" is the denial of the frailty of their humanity." -Patti Flinn

My mental health took a huge hit as soon as reality set in that I had literally become a single mother. No, not just single, I mean "single single," that "you ain't getting no support from me if I don't have you" type single. Yep, you know before a relationship ends you go through the "maybe's" and the "what if's" and the "but it could work out's." But when reality sets in that it's really done and you have to process how to get through it all alone, you start to ask yourself "how the hell am I going to do this?" Well this was me. I went from being a wife, to a part-time lover - or in other words, his side chick - to a complete single mother all as a result of me saying "No" and putting myself first.

Now you may wonder why I said no and I must admit, that's a good question because time and time again I asked myself that very same question. I mean I had it "good enough," right? I had a little time from my husband and my baby had a little time seeing his dad. So why say no? Why did I mess up a decent thing? Is "good enough" really enough? It wasn't for me. I finally decided enough was enough. I was done with the back and forth, with coming second, with being an option and I was no longer going to be the victim of destruction, abuse and self-sabotage. Unfortunately, I could see a family pattern and I sure was not going to repeat the cycle of generational curses I had witnessed in my life first-hand.

Yes, before putting me first I struggled with an identity crisis, trying to figure out who I was and how to go through this journey with absolutely no support from the father of my child. See, I was always a pretty confident woman who was secure in who I was; yet, at this moment, I was in the midst of an identity crisis. Single mom, divorced, early 30's, and my baby had to eat. Honestly, I didn't even know who the heck I was, but I had to figure it out. How was I supposed to raise a little boy by myself? A little brown one at that.

I've constantly heard "other women have done it before you and they have done it well," or "you're strong just like your grandma/mama/aunties/etc. were," but baby, I didn't want to be strong. If I'm being quite honest, I didn't have the strength to do anything more than just show up, because everything else in me mentally and emotionally had checked out. But how could this be? How could Andrea Joie' just be showing up, but not showing out? I have always been the role model, leader, businesswoman, the "tell it like it is" one, the one that "didn't take no shit" (excuse my French), the strong one or "superwoman," but who was I to call when I needed someone to lean on? I am a natural born leader and overachiever, but eventually I realized I was doing to myself what I had seen done to the other women in my family: self-sabotaging. I was expecting perfection from an imperfect person. I hated being on the sidelines and struggling with managing my mental health. I am a problem solver, period. I don't have problems.

I became embarrassed and I had no idea where to turn. This journey became one that quickly began molding me into the woman I needed to be rather than the one everyone thought I was. The mask had to come off. My vulnerability had begun to show. I could no longer be that perfect picture my family and friends saw me as. I could no longer be this expected "superwoman" that hid behind the mask, but rather, I had to learn to be okay with showing the softer side of myself that many thought didn't exist. In order to do this, however, I began seeing a therapist and she began reading me like a book. There were many unhealed past traumas that I needed to address that I was obviously covering up with this "superwoman syndrome." I had to learn to forgive my past abusers and most of all, myself. I had to learn how to let up off myself and make a more conscious effort to embrace the freedom of screwing up. Now, I honestly even find humor in my screw-ups sometimes. It surely beats self-castigation; I tell you that.

I want to be clear about who I am and many of my flaws so that others will understand when I tell my story. It's not for sympathy, but for understanding that any of us can struggle with wearing a mask and sometimes even the cape just to cover up our real feelings. Anxiety and depression, they are real. I have and sometimes still do experience them both. And even if it's only for a short period of time, a struggle is a struggle. No matter how you learn to cope with it, understand, some things never go away. You're entitled to feel how you feel, but you are not entitled to make excuses for not getting back up for you. The healing is not for your family. It's not for your child(ren). It's not even for generations to come. It's for you. Stop thinking you alone must change the world or your family, because you don't. You are human and you too will experience things you have to learn to cope with in your own way and that's okay. Take the time you need to cope, recognize your triggers, and understand "No" is not only a complete sentence, but it's also your beginning of someone else's ending. You don't need validation from the world, a spouse, an ex, or even family to live as you choose. Be unapologetic in your decisions. CHOOSE YOU!!!

"I am human. I am imperfect. I make mistakes. I sometimes need help. The authenticity necessary to acknowledge these truths is my only superpower." -Stephanie Pearson-Davis

We are all fascinated by superheroes. They go above and beyond what the world considers reasonable to fight wars that aren't even theirs and save people that aren't even their assignment. As women, we rarely ever really internalize the concept that we don't have to do it all and the world has to internalize this as well. Unfortunately, many times we pass this on to our girls as well as influence our boys that women are "super women." Of course, as a single mother, I've learned to rig house repairs, invented foods that were strict in budget to stretch limited funds, picked myself up off the bed even during my sickest moments to feed my baby, work a full-time job, and run a business full time, just to come home to cook, clean and entertain a six-year-old on a daily. I've done all these things, because as a woman, we often feel obligated. Ladies, let's face it, we make this look easy, right? We do so much with so little. Unfortunately, women don't get to separate any aspects of life. Work life bleeds into home life which bleeds into social life. They all teeter precariously like a giant balancing tame just waiting on one thing to fall over. But it doesn't have to be this way. Everything is not our fault or responsibility - not family, not relationships, day-to-day stressors, nope…those are not on us. I guarantee, trading that "strong" title for a little bit of help is certainly okay.

I didn't know how to ask for help at first, but people in my life helped me. In the past, I would let most conversations "go in one ear and out the other" especially when people told me I was being too hard on myself, but I've learned to actually consider what is said. I learned to ask myself what I would say to another person in my situation. If I determine I would show them compassion, I would try to give that to myself. Per usual, I'm serving the truth on a hot platter. Feel free to eat as you may.

"The ultimate irony is that it is easier for us to be kinder to others than to ourselves." -Patti Flinn

Understand, your projection of yourself and the perfect picture of what you believe motherhood and marriage or a relationship should be will harm your mental and emotional health if you let it. So, you ask, what should you do?

Here are a few pieces of advice:
- Stop pursuing perfection and only chase progress.
- Let people know when their expectations are unreasonable.
- Be transparent and know that it's okay to ask for help.
- Teach your children that mama is good, but she's not God. Rest is necessary.
- Repeat positive affirmations and prayers.
- Stop neglecting yourself. Self-care such as nails, hair, and time away is necessary.
- HEAL…get the help you need. Therapy is okay (highly recommended).
- The word "No" is a complete sentence. No need to explain or justify…NO MEANS NO!!!

As Chaka Khan says in her song "I'm Every Woman" - "I'm every woman, it's all in me, anything you want done baby, I do it naturally." Naturally, we try to be everything for everyone but maybe the key to changing the superwoman syndrome is to change within ourselves and then change the way we (women) are viewed to the world. This isn't the land of make-believe and you don't have the ability to fly to the tallest building and save the world no matter what others may think of you. You don't have to have an "S on your chest," beautiful. You are not invincible. Do not internalize the words "superwoman" and think you can't stop and take the time you need for you. You do not have to do it all, alone.

I strive to be the greatest example, for me, for other women and for my son, but being honest, I struggle at times and even sometimes fail; yet, I survive and I manage. Though I'm not everyone's SUPER woman, I am A WOMAN, and that is enough. I AM ENOUGH. Just being me is my "superpower." No mask necessary.

Amazon's Best-Selling Author, Andrea Joie', also known as "Crickets Mommy," is a single mother to a dinosaur loving little boy, owner of Nested Grace Doula, a radio host, model, and a model mom. She was born and raised a country girl in a small town named Farmers Union, the sticks of NC.

She's also a proud member of The Cape Fear Band of Skaruré and Woccon Indians "Swamp Indians". When she is not outdoors fishing, hunting, at a racetrack or just being barefoot and dirty, Andrea spends most of her time in front of a camera, reading, shopping, traveling the world, or enjoying good food and music. An admitted sports fanatic, she absolutely loves her Carolina Panthers and Boston Celtics.

Andrea is also a graduate of Campbell University's School of Pharmacy and Health Sciences and currently practices Industrial Pharmacy. She developed her love for writing as a therapy of expression, determined to find her happy ending – even if she had to write it.
Andrea currently lives in Rocky Mount, NC with her little Paleontologist in the making "Cricket" and "the animals".

Keep in touch with her via the web:
Website: www.andreajoie.com
Facebook and Instagram: @andreajoie

Acknowledgements

Megan Cotton
Dapper Xpressions
www.dapperxpressions.com
Facebook: @dapperxpressions
Instagram: @dapperxpressions

Alaric Hopkins
Quality A Cuts

KiEsha Spaulding

DONJA HARPER
HYPER REEL FILMWORKS
d-harper0211.wixsite.com/website
Facebook: @hyperreelfilms

Ursula McGrew
Facebook: @tatersgigi

Anthony Stanback
Stanback Photography
www.stanbackphotography.com
Instagram: @stansolutionsphotography

Morgan Lambert
Morgan Lambert
Facebook:@morganlambert
Instagram: @heartless_lynn

Ponchitta Spaulding

Cliff Vasser
Vasser Trucking

Brita Spaulding

Jordan Manley
Facebook: @wise_btlr

Nika Spaulding
Instagram: @xx_spaulding

Amiez Rowecooper
Grandiose , Inc.
www.grandiosecreations.com
Facebook: @grandiosegrandiose
Instagram: @grandiose

Ashley Armstrong
AMA Art
https://linktr.ee/amaart14

Stacey and Stefan Williams

BRIAN BOYD
Instagram: bb_brianboyd

Antonio Clark
Instagram: @professoraltc

Amanda Cutchin
Facebook: @AmandaCutchin

William Manley
Manley's Photography
Facebook: William Manley
Instagram: @manleys_photography

Quamane Smith
Facebook: @QuaMane Smith
Instagram: @Mane34__

The Cape Was a Load On My Back
Ursula Jones

Being a mother automatically requires you to be a Superwoman. Some mothers are even our adult children's Superwoman. I am one of those mothers. I have four children. One of my children has a mental illness, Bipolar Disorder. She requires a lot of my time, attention, understanding, patience, and me going above and beyond the call of duty. There are many times when I'm exhausted and emotionally drained, but it's difficult for me to say no or not take a call because I don't know what state of mind she's in, what she might do if I don't answer, or if she's safe. I cry often because I often feel that I'm on the clock 24 hours a day.

Philippians 4:6: Don't worry about anything; instead pray about everything. Tell God what you need, and thank him for all he has done.

I need God. Every day. Every moment. Every second that I breathe, I need God. I am not strong enough on my own. I am not your Superwoman. I live with this everyday as earlier in my life, I wanted to throw the cape away. The load was too heavy for me. And the more I tried to be that Superwoman, I was hurting myself.

It all started when my oldest daughter, Cedina, was about in the fourth grade. I had so many problems with her because she was so hyper and she wouldn't listen to the teachers. It had gotten so bad that the school nurse wanted me to get her some help. In other words, put her on medication so it would slow her down. As she got older, it got worse. She didn't want to listen or do anything the teachers said. At that time, her dad, Cedric, and I just put in our heads that we had a bad child - just being honest. We couldn't handle her and we knew we had to do something because it was getting bad. Once she got in high school, they kicked her out of school and placed her in the alternative school. Her dad and I tried to get help from the principal because she was Cedric's cousin and we thought maybe she would help us knowing the condition we dealt with. Instead, she informed us that we needed to get help for her before it got any worse.

Well, my son's father, Ray, who was my boyfriend at the time got a job offer in Texarkana, Arkansas. Ray, the kids and I all left and moved to Arkansas for two years, leaving my home in Kemptown, NC empty until we were to return. Once we made it to AR and got the children enrolled in school a few days later, my daughter started the same mess. Once again, she ended up out of school. Now this was a load for me. We stayed in a twin city so across the street was Texarkana, Texas. There was another chance she could go to school on the Texas side. You wouldn't believe it, but she got kicked out of that school too and the next and final option was Job Corps. This was an option I hated to do because my daughter had never stayed away from home and I was terrified that she had to go. After all her paperwork was straightened out, she was sent off and I hated it. I was so mad I wanted to move back home and just deal with this situation in North Carolina, but I knew I couldn't.

After a few months, Ray and I got married there in Arkansas. He later got laid off from that job and we went back home to NC and Cedina was left in Little Rock, Arkansas where she was settled in at Job Corps. She hated it there and would call me every day wanting to come home but there was nothing I could do until she finished. After she completed the program, I was so happy and glad to have her home because she was 18 by this time and I figured she had had time to grow and things would be different now. Well, she sure fooled me. After a while, she got worse again. Ray was called to go to another job and this time I stayed home with the children. One night she walked in my room and told me she should kill me and at that very moment, I decided to no longer ignore the signs of her mental illness. I went to get her help the next day because she couldn't even remember she had done this. After she was diagnosed with paranoid bipolar schizophrenia, I started her on monthly injections to manage her episodes because I knew she hated taking pills and wasn't going to take them anyway. I also secured her an apartment that was on the way into town so I had to pass by there every day and I checked on her.

I was so relieved I was able to rest a little. But then one day she met this guy and they became really close. She moved him right in with her and he ended up getting her kicked out of her place. Now she was back to square one. Again, my husband Ray got another job offer and it was long-term so that meant us moving with him to Texas again in 2015. The property manager gave Cedina a date to move and she didn't want to come to TX but she had no choice. My best friend, Melissa, was coming to Texas for her birthday weekend so I had Cedina to fly with her. When Cedina arrived, God knows she had me so stressed with her mood swings. She hated TX and wanted to move back to NC. While I did want her to stay in TX to be close to me, I honestly did not want her to stay with us. She finally got approved for her next apartment and my son helped her get back to NC and moved in.

For more than three years she did well until she stopped going to get her injections. After that, her mind had her seeing things that weren't there and all kinds of things. That same guy she had met before got her kicked out again and this time she said, "I'm not moving back with you. I will stay on the streets before I go back to Texas." And that's exactly what she did. When I heard my daughter was actually living on the streets, I flew down to NC in the middle of the pandemic to try and get her to fly back with me but she would not leave. She was about 100 pounds. I cried because I had never seen her so thin in my life. She was pushing a buggy and had all the little bits of belongings in it. I begged her and even cried in her face but she said "Ma, I'm going to be alright. I don't want to be in Texas. I wish you could move back home." It hurt my heart because as a wife I knew I had an obligation to be by my husband, but my child was out here in the streets and she needed me. Before leaving, I tried to get the authorities to pick her up and admit her but they kept telling me she wasn't a threat to herself. For months I couldn't sleep. I ate up everything I could to hide the depression and I even hid it from my husband. I prayed so much that God would turn this mess around and bless my baby until I stopped praying. I was tired. This Superwoman I appeared to be was about to explode.

One day I got a call that my daughter was seen walking all the way from Fayetteville, NC to Tarheel, NC, which is about 25 miles. Finally, she stopped at a gas station and the young lady that was working was one of my ex-coworkers who remembered when I used to talk about my daughter's illness all the time. She called me and said "your daughter is here and she's dripping wet sitting at the table." I asked her if she could please watch her while I work on getting her some help. I called on my best friend Melissa again because I knew she would do anything for me and she knew how much I loved my daughter. She had to go to the sheriff's office and fill out paperwork to get her admitted. I knew that they would keep her because they had records of when she had been previously admitted because of her illness. Once I knew she was admitted I was able to sleep. God, I thank you. My daughter had been homeless for about a year - not because she didn't have anywhere to stay, but because she went without her meds. She got back on her injections and was well again. It took months for the injections to settle back in her system. Once they were, she was getting back to normal. She now has her own place, a roof over her head; thank God! It's walking distance to the store. She has a therapist who checks on her every month and she gets her injections every month. By the grace of God, she is stable.

You see, I wanted to wear that cape and handle everything on my own, but God had it all worked out another way. When I wanted to give up, He said hold on. My daughter went through the whole pandemic and thank God, she never caught COVID. She was around lots of strangers and never got sick, thank God. He had His angels watching over my baby the whole time. So now I say, no I'm Not Your Superwoman, but I am a Super Woman!

Ursula Jones is a native of Council, NC and currently resides in Lake Jackson, Texas. She is married to Ray Jones and is the mother of four beautiful children and six grandchildren. Ursula is the Founder and Owner of RJ Cleaning Services LLC and a Notary/Loan Signing Agent in the state of TX. Ursula loves traveling, prioritizing her family, shopping and living life to the fullest. God is the head of her life and she knows through Him all things are possible. She trusts His plan for her life and allows Him to guide her footsteps to GREATER.

Learn more about Ursula by visiting her website or connecting with her on social media.

Facebook: Ursula Chancy Jones
Instagram: @prissy_jones
linktr.ee/prissy_jones35

Acknowledgements

Joann Bellamy
Joannsjourney
www.joannsjourney.com
Facebook: Joann Bellamy

Our Capes May Have Holes, But We Can Still Fly

Lorna Kelley

December 21st, 2013 was the day my life threw me for a complete and utter, surprising, beyond my wildest dreams, a never could I have ever imagined LOOP!

I was living with my fiancé. This would be my second shot at marriage since my first marriage did not work out years prior. My first husband and I were young and dumb and didn't know a thing, nothing, nada, zilch about what it took to make a marriage work. Fortunately, fate allowed me to find love again with my soul mate, the person who "got me". We had been dating for over eight years and I finally took the plunge and moved into his place that summer with plans to get married the following year.

Now this is where it gets tricky: I was 43 years old with three children who were 24, 19 and 14 years old. I could taste being an empty-nester. I was a few short years away from what I imagined to be a life of pursuing new hobbies, lounging and traveling. I imagined myself reading books by the pool at some all-inclusive resort, or maybe going back to school, or just whatever. I was looking forward to Me Time. Well, you know what God says about plans right? "HE laughs at them!" On this fateful day, after being a week late, I took a pregnancy test, and well, you can probably guess the rest. Yes, at 43 years old, with almost all grown children, I was pregnant. The very next emotion was the greatest wave of fear I have ever felt in my life.

Google became my best friend and my worst enemy. I spent HOURS combing through various sites. My searches included key phrases like "43 and pregnant" and "risks of having a baby at midlife" and the dreaded "geriatric pregnancy". I'm an analytical person so I wanted all the stats, stories, any information I could get. I literally spent hours at my computer.

My fiancé Ben, who is now my husband, was ecstatic. He had no children, so when I sat on the couch next to him and showed him the pregnancy test with two lines, he was soooo excited! He hugged and kissed me and said "it better be a boy!" He so wanted a son. As for me, I just wanted a healthy baby and to live through delivery. OMG, the pressure was on!

The next day I made an appointment with my OBGYN and when they asked for my birthday, I was certain they would immediately rush me in. In my mind, this was a medical emergency! Seriously, I only knew ONE other person who had a baby naturally at my age. The receptionist who set my appointment did absolutely nothing out of the ordinary - no gasps, no ambulance was sent, no rushed same-day appointment. Apparently, the urgency was all in my head.

The next nine months were riddled with intense all day morning sickness, ultrasounds every month, many "geriatric pregnancy" screenings and high-risk medical protocols. Ben was a pillar of support. He became a regular at our local pharmacy bringing home over-the-counter remedies to help ease my sickness. At the time, I was also working a high-pressured corporate sales job with demanding quotas and responsibilities that required me to travel. I was essentially a sick road warrior, swollen, scared, worried and stressed. It was A LOT. Eight months into my pregnancy, I begged my doctor to approve short-term disability. At one of my many appointments I cried and pleaded for him to please let me go out on leave early. He finally gave his approval and granted my leave which allowed me to focus on my health and the health of my baby.

Fast forward to today. I am now a 50+ year old mother with an energetic, inquisitive eight-year-old. My son has taught me the most valuable lessons about myself and about life. As a mature woman raising a small child, I have the capacity, wisdom and experience to see things from a different perspective, a much clearer perspective than I did as a mother in my younger years. With my older children, I was young, trying to find my way, build a life, have a social life, navigate through a tough marriage and ultimately a divorce. My life at that time was a whirlwind. I was literally just running from one task to the next. I wasn't living, I was simply existing. It sounds cliché, but that's what it was.

Having a child later in life has taught me the greatest lessons. It's taught me strength, compassion, patience and I get to see the world through my young son's eyes. Of course, I worry sometimes about the future. What will he think of me once he realizes I'm so much older than his friends' mothers? Will he be ashamed of me and tell me to wait in the car at school events? Will I live long enough to see my little boy's children? I quickly snap out of this mindset, because I realize - you know what? Tomorrow is promised to no woman. We're making the best of each moment, just the two of us. I try to make sure our experiences are meaningful. I choose quality over quantity in regards to our time. We play board games for hours, go to concerts, shows, museums and parks. I savor each and every second with him because I want each one to count. I want to make good memories.

My contribution to this book is certainly not about pregnancy, being a mother, wife, friend, co-worker and business owner. That is really not that noteworthy. Millions of women do it every day. However, what I would like to share with you are some of the things I've learned along the way as a result of this unpredictable life event and the first is: time is precious. What can make the biggest difference in our well-being as women is not what we do - though life is indeed full of responsibilities - but it is certainly about HOW we do it. I've learned that if something does not provide peace of mind, joy, fulfillment and/or well-being, it's just not worth it. If a relationship, whether personal, professional or romantic, becomes toxic, do what you need to do to fix it. If that doesn't work, let it go.

As women, it's important to understand that our individual journeys are meant to bring us to a destination. Driving down a road endlessly without a destination is a waste of time. Ultimately, if we are open, we can drive our life toward a path of fulfillment and joy. How do we do that? We do that by learning from the lessons, by reflecting, meditating, exercising, praying, eating right, reading, listening, watching and again, LEARNING. I implore you to get around women that inspire you to reach for higher levels. Get around some like-minded women you aspire to be like. Join groups, meetups, conferences and mastermind classes that will help elevate your thinking. Read books about business, networking, tax laws, raising powerful children, investing and other topics that interest you. Find a good therapist to help guide you through the work and heal childhood trauma, because we all are essentially trying to heal that hurt little girl inside. Pinpoint that moment in your childhood that defines your trauma. We all have one or two of those moments that are permeated in our memories. Work through these moments through meditation, prayer, self-help books and a good therapist. Like Iyanla Vanzant says, "Do the work Beloved." We must indeed do the work. On the other side of the work is where peace, joy, contentment, fulfillment and success can be found.

My little miracle child will be nine this year and it has been one of the hardest, if not THE hardest challenge of my life. While my peers are off enjoying traveling, concerts and discovering new hobbies, I'm immersed in Roblox, Minecraft and whatever comes up as the latest kids' obsession. I'm not sure if my little boy is keeping me young or if he is the cause of my increasing number of gray hairs! What I do know is that this chapter in my life has taught me so much about myself. It has shown me how strong women really are, but even more importantly, it has taught me how to ask for help. There is no way I could get anything done without the support of my husband, mother-in-law, other family members, friends and my mommy groups. I discovered early that it really does take a village. The cool thing about social media is that there is a "village" waiting at your fingertips. For those who may not have family or friends nearby, one can use social media and meetup groups to create a village. Seek out champions within your village. Select one or two key people from your support system that are your go-to's - people who are in your corner and have a willingness to help. In return, shower those people with love and appreciation.

I laugh when I think about it now, but there was a time when my husband and I brought our little boy on EVERY vacation. I mean even couples' trips. There we were, the only couple with our child in tow. I just could not leave him, and in addition, I felt it was important for him to have stamps in his passport! However, I received some wise counsel from a very good friend who said "Lorna, it's okay, your baby boy will be okay. You need to have fun and take some trips with just you and your husband." She was right. My husband and I started taking a few mini trips throughout the year without our child. It rejuvenated our marriage and allowed us some down time. We gave ourselves permission to reset and recharge. Sometimes it's just a weekend, a short road trip a couple of hours away, to see a concert or show, but it's enough time to clear our minds and reconnect. This is why I love to have a network of those around, as part of my village, who provide wise counsel. Find a couple of women who can impart wisdom into your life. Accept that you don't know everything. So much growth happens when you surround yourself with the right people.

So yes, our capes may be torn in some spots and may even have a few holes here or there. Our capes may be stained with blood, sweat and many tears. You may have experienced incredible loss, such as the death of a child, husband or parent. You may have been fired from your job, lost out on a well-deserved promotion or had a business fail; yet, you are still flying, soaring, expanding and reaching new heights. Women continue to move in powerful ways. We are heads of corporations, owners of multiple businesses, educated, beautiful and powerful. We do it all, but it's important to remember that we can't do it alone. We need a support system. Our health, minds, bodies and souls depend on these important connections. We also need to remember that "NO" is a complete sentence. It's okay to not try to be all things to all people. Hang onto the cape, the cape is good. It is our super power, but we need to be mindful to mend the holes with self-care and love. Restore your cape by embarking on an intentional journey to healing.

Keep flying Sis. You've got this.

Lorna Kelley is a native of Ottawa, Canada and has made her home in Virginia with her husband and children for over twenty years. This dynamic, complex serial entrepreneur is passionate about empowering women, and particularly women in business, towards a journey of better health, healing, love and light.

Lorna is the founder and CEO of Virginia Natural Beauty LLC, which was created by combining Kelley's love for fashion, fitness and all things natural! She is passionate about empowering individuals to be their best, especially women. Ms. Kelley believes that, "Although beauty really does start from within, when we look good, we feel good. When we feel good, we do good and I want to help others feel good about who they are, naturally."

Furthermore, she is the CEO and founder of Yummy Properties, a property investment company, where she invests in rental properties in Richmond, VA and surrounding areas.

In 2021, after working with a national medical practice, Lorna fell in love with being an advocate for the underserved senior population. She works as a trusted advisor to help bridge the medical services gap, educating patients on how to gain access to much needed healthcare resources. She founded First Choice Senior Solutions and also Lorna Kelley Insurance to help address those needs. She works passionately and tirelessly with seniors in her community.

My Journey to Learning I Am Not Your Superwoman!

Kisha Lesane

My name is Kisha Lesane and food is my life. Okay, let me explain: I am a passionate food blogger who has a stunning personality, a winning smile and the appetite to match. My number one motto is "butter makes everything better."

I am from a small quaint country town in North Carolina where I promise everyone knows everyone's name. Food is a staple at every visit with friends and family. Sweet tea is always in the fridge and someone has a cake or pie on the table. My fondest memories are at my great-grandma's house on Emma Street where she always had Hoop Cheese, a sharp cheese with a red ring around it, and Ginger Snaps cookies on the table. She also had a pot of something warm and filling on the stove. The good food didn't just stop after her passing. Instead, the torch was passed down to my grandma, who without any effort, was always able to create a great meal before her passing and then it was passed down to my dad. I watched my dad and family run a successful restaurant and club together and when all the customers were gone, I watched the joy on my dad's face while he was in the kitchen. Watching those magical moments awakened my love for food, restaurants and more, but this story is not all unicorns and rainbows, so let me tell you more about that.

Six years ago, I lost every worldly possession I owned besides a gold Honda Accord. I was no longer in contact with what I considered to be my heart beats outside my chest. Losing contact with them was the biggest hurt I ever experienced and I still battle with that loss in my heart. I really didn't have much time to process the hurt because during this time I had to learn how to sleep in my car at night when I couldn't afford a hotel room, while still showing up for work every day with a smile and looking fresh. I was determined to rebuild my life and prove I had what it took to make it. I grew stronger, or at least that's what I told myself every day. I must admit, I became a pro at looking like I had it together when on the inside, I was really falling apart.

As heartbreaking and disappointing as that time in my life was, it still didn't prepare me for the agonizing pain I felt when I really lost myself. After finally rebuilding everything after the first loss six years ago, I had a new place to call home in Atlanta, Georgia. This was a huge goal to finally move to Georgia so I could be in the place that would help my business succeed as a food blogger. I also had a car that I was able to make payments for on time (which was a big deal for me), an amazing job, a dog that adored me, plus more. I even had what I knew then as love. I thought I was on top of the world. Then one day it all changed. There was a fire in my home and everything I had worked hard to rebuild to be able to finally say I was getting back on track was simply turned into ashes.

I knew I could keep going because I had done this before, right? Oh how wrong I was. I lost my energy to survive anymore. I thought this world would be better without me. I felt lost inside. It seemed once again I was on a Ferris wheel that just kept going around and dang it, I wanted off. See, as I was picking up the pieces I still had to show up and be a productive employee at my job at Atlantic Station in Atlanta. I was picking up extra shifts anytime they asked. I said yes because I knew what it felt like to not be able to afford a hotel and I told myself I wouldn't do that part again. The fact was I needed the money so I pushed myself hard and even though I was burning the candle at both ends, I still had to smile and provide excellent customer service. I was working hard to get a promotion at my job at the time. As an entrepreneur, I was also still expected to run my business, return emails, and be consistent on social media. It was my business and its success was my responsibility. I didn't care how tired I was because I had put so much hard work into building my business, my brand and my life and I refused to quit, no matter how hard life was at the time. I was trying hard every day to remain positive. Back then, however, it was a chore to even think about finding the good in anything. Every day was about survival.

On top of trying to push through everyday life challenges, I even had a moment in my life where I allowed myself to be abused and manipulated. I was told things like "no one will ever love you," or my favorite one was "you will never succeed or ever be anything" by someone I felt I could finally let my guard down around and be completely vulnerable with. Imagine looking at yourself in the mirror in that hotel room before heading to work and thinking: how much more can I take before I completely throw in the towel? I remember during that time in my life I felt like I took my heart out of my chest and handed it to him because he convinced me he was in my life to make me better. In truth, I needed to make myself better and it was my duty to love myself. I no longer place any blame on the individual who made those comments or used his hands on me to make me listen because let's be honest, I used to feel this way about myself. I had already told myself that I was useless every day and I used to believe I was not worthy of love and he just mirrored what I saw in me.

I had no idea that sometimes it's okay to stop and start over. Walking away did not mean failure. I had to learn that with love and with life. Once I started the healing process, I also had to remind myself that his behavior was a reflection on himself, not me. To this day, I find myself always apologizing because I'm scared I'm doing something wrong. I have grown more aware and I look for validation sometimes, even when it's not needed. I know this will take time to overcome but I'm dedicated to putting in the work. The beauty in this story is my shift in perspective. I now know I had to forgive myself to truly heal. Now I can honestly say I do find the positive in all I do, though it was a journey getting to this place. I no longer float through the day just trying to survive. One of the steps of my healing process was understanding how much power was behind the word "No!"

I began saying no to tolerating less than I deserved. Saying no to not feeling guilty for putting my phone on Do Not Disturb when I needed to. I used to deeply believe that no matter what you were going through you had to show up for others' needs. If they asked, you must show up or you would be considered selfish. Well guess what? That is completely wrong. This one was extremely hard to accept no matter how many times my therapist drilled it in my head when I started my healing. Finally, it clicked when I was on a plane and the flight attendant said to all of us "in the event of an emergency, be sure to place your oxygen mask on first before helping your neighbor." Sounds like a simple statement, right? Well it made me sit straight up and realize, *Kisha, you have been pouring from an empty cup and everyone you love deserves the best of you and that is not what you have been giving.*

Saying no to limiting myself to what society thinks is a sign of success was a power move I wish I learned sooner. I always believed success was a nice car and a big house. I grew up thinking success was finding a powerfully rich husband who pays the bills. It didn't matter how he treated me or how he made me feel, as long as bills were paid. Instead, I worked hard to place myself in a position where I can take care of myself and be in love with someone who makes me laugh, brings out the best in me and pushes me with a gentle hand to be strong. What he brings to the table is an addition. If I hadn't learned that it's okay for me to do what I thought was best for me, I would have never applied to a job that has me living on the road 320 days out of the year, which is a dream come true for me. All my life I wanted to travel the world and try new experiences outside of my hometown, but most importantly, while loving what I do and I have that with this job. Even now as I write my story I am sitting on a rooftop bar with an incredible fruity drink in hand in a beautiful city I would have never traveled to otherwise! I know this may seem small to some, but to someone who has slept in her Honda before, I never dreamt this was even possible. I now have the opportunity to be flown to a new city every 30 to 60 days for work. I finally get paid to experience culinary cultural experiences for my business while promoting exceptional customer service as part of my job and seeing a whole new world I didn't even realize existed. This is in no way a brag. This is proof that learning to say no will open so many doors.

This southern girl from a small town who endured the worst of the worst that life had to offer, somehow found enough strength to stand strong to say "I deserve to be happy, full of peace and I have the power to say NO!" Finding the courage to remain committed to myself has opened my world to be the best me I can be.

"Hope rises like a Phoenix from the ashes of shattered dreams." -S.A. Sachs

Kisha Lesane

Kisha Lesane is an influencer, YouTuber, Vlogger and published author from a small, quaint town in North Carolina. Recognizing her love for food, Kisha decided to turn her passion into a thriving business when she launched A Pinch of Butter LLC in 2019. Her motto is "butter makes everything better" and as a blogger, she finds joy in experiencing new restaurants, drinks and products which she shares with her followers on her digital platforms. Moreover, as a Task Force Front Desk Supervisor, she has the opportunity to travel nearly 320 days out of the year and experience cultural cuisine all over the world while working the front desk of some amazing hotels.

Keep in touch with Kisha:

www.apinchofbutter.com
www.Facebook.com/PinchButter
www.Instagram.com/a_pinch_of_butter/
www.Twitter.com/PinchButter/

Choosing Me...Intentionally
Tynesha Marie

"Intentional living is the art of making our own choices before others' choices make us."
— Richie Norton

What am I going to feed my family, I have to pick up a birthday gift for my daughter's friend, or my son's friend, or somebody's friend, I would love to participate, Oh I forgot I have to drop these bags off to the Goodwill, Yes I will volunteer for field day, Let's do a playdate, Oh, let me log-in to check a few more emails to get ahead, Oh I'll do it, What am I going to wear to my husband's work event, Yes, I will serve on the PTO board, Oh no, I forgot that ingredient for tonight's dinner, I will be there, How can I support you, Sign me up, What do you need, What do you need, What do you need...... BUT WHAT ABOUT WHAT I NEED?

That first paragraph does not make any sense, does it? No periods, not even a semicolon, just a continuation of things I was doing and things I felt like I had to do, and nothing, not one thing had anything to do with pouring into myself. I purposely started my story off like that because that was how I was operating pre-pandemic. I was giving so much of myself to others and thought I was doing an excellent job, and some may say I was. There were so many times I have been called a superwoman and guess what? I LOVED IT! I wore that title like a badge of honor and I took it as the ultimate compliment when family, friends, and associates called me 'superwoman.'

I thought that I was killing it, and again, some may say I was, but at what and whose expense?

I did not realize how much pressure that compliment inadvertently put on me if I am being honest. There have been countless times that I have said that I was 'fine,' but I was not. While I was focused on being a superwoman, I had become overweight. I was not trying to eat healthy for real or even exercise seriously. At that time, I was a loose natural and I did not have time or the energy to take care of my hair, so it eventually started shedding more than it should have been. While I was pouring into everyone and everything else, and making them a priority, I was not pouring into myself. I was not doing anything that was just for me. But isn't that what I was supposed to do? Wasn't I supposed to give of myself unselfishly and serve others?

I cannot quite pinpoint how my mission in life turned into being everything to everyone and not asking for help. When I finally did ask for help, I would sometimes micromanage the hell out of it. For example, my husband and kids DO NOT fold clothes the way that I do and the way that I do it is "right," right? ABSOLUTELY NOT! I remember telling the kids repeatedly how to fold clothes "the right way" or I would go behind my husband and re-fold their clothes when they were babies. I know, crazy. When I decided to let that go, I felt so much better because 1) the clothes get ironed anyway, and 2) who is looking in the drawers and closets in this house judging how clothes are folded? And if anyone has done that, shame on you! But I digress...

I rarely said no to anyone or anything; it was always 'yes.' I would make myself available to others, while I was neglecting myself. I wanted to say 'no' so many times, but did I dare let people think I did not support them or did not love them enough to show up? I could not do that because that is not what you do for your loved ones and it always seemed as if there was something to do. Consequently, I remember being frustrated all the time and drained of energy. And then I always felt disappointed when people did not *seem* to value my efforts of showing up, because hell, I was working my behind off just to be there. How dare they not value my precious time of supporting them?

Moreover, I have seen so many women doing the exact same thing I was doing: being everything to everyone, while treating themselves as an afterthought. I am a 39-year-old Black female, a wife for 15 years, and the mother of two beautiful kids – one daughter and one son. I am a middle child with an older brother and a younger sister. We grew up in a single-parent home with our mother, while our maternal grandparents and Uncle Buster lived upstairs.

As previously stated, I cannot pinpoint when my mission in life was to be everything to everyone, but in hindsight, I believe that it has been in me since I was little, generational even. My granny was a caregiver and I think unbeknownst to my mother, she became one because of that. For almost forty years, I watched my mommy unselfishly giving her time and resources to others while forgoing her personal needs and dreams. Now that I think about it, did my mommy even have any dreams?

I remember being little when my mommy finally got a job working full-time overnight, 11 pm – 7 am, so that she could care for my brother, sister, and me during the day, plus run errands. It wasn't just us she was caring for though. She also helped care for my uncle Lewis who was diagnosed with Lupus and fought it for so many years. Countless times she would get off work and take him to a doctor's appointment with no sleep. Eventually, he lost that battle (but won the victory!).

My mommy played a major role in helping to raise most of my nieces, taking them to and from school to help my brother and sister-in-law out while he worked and she went to school for nursing. Again, doing this while working the graveyard shift and with very little sleep. She would then eventually become my grandad's caretaker until he eventually passed away. And then, there was my granny. When my granny's health took a turn for the worst, my mommy had to bathe her, feed her, take her to the bathroom, and fight with my granny at doctors' appointments. My granny definitely told doctors what she would and would not do. Eventually, God called her home.

All I know is to give to others and neglect myself. I hate to call it a generational curse because I admired my granny and mommy for their love and desire to care for others. But do I want my daughter, my Sweet Pea, to live like that? Neglecting herself? No! She has been watching me since she came into this world and I needed to do better and model better for her. She needed to know that self-care is a priority and not just an afterthought, if it was even a thought at all. But how was I going to do this? I was in deep with being on the go and overextending myself with people and activities. I wanted better but just did not know how to do better.

And then, March of 2020 came, and the world shut completely down. Schools closed for the remainder of the academic year as teachers were unfairly tasked with still trying to engage their students. I remember my son crying on the phone with his teacher when she called and told him that she would not be able to see him for the remainder of the school year. I cried too. That was the same year my daughter was graduating from the fifth grade. Although she liked her teacher, she was happy she never had to go back to her elementary school; my daughter is wired differently. However, my husband and I wanted to see her walk across the stage and accept her diploma. But that moment never came and that broke my heart.

Most businesses shut down, which forced millions of people to either lose their job or work from home and the world quickly realized who the REAL essential workers were. The news reported daily on how millions of people were dying from the coronavirus. The world was grieving. I too was grieving. Yet, the year in which a virus was taking so many people's breath away, was the year I was finally able to freely breathe.

I did not have to "rip and run" as my mommy and granny would say. I had time to think and to just be and I loved it. I eventually got back into doing things that I once enjoyed doing, such as reading books. What is most amazing was that during this time, I had my 'aha' moment and rediscovered who I was at my core and really figured out what matters most to me. And although I had always known it, my life pre-pandemic had so many distractions. I had experienced loss before, but to grieve for so many people that I did not know daily because of a virus.... my God, that was different. I realized how I was going to operate moving forward. With every fiber in my body, I would strive to live a life of abundance because that is what God promised me. And when I say abundance, I do not mean rich, although that would be nice. When I say abundance, I mean fulfillment. And so now, I am on a mission.

Today, my theme for my life is to *be intentional* with my relationship with God, family, friends, my community, but most importantly, myself. I no longer wish to do things that no longer align with... well, heck, if I just do not want to do something, I am more comfortable with saying no. I still give my time to others and I am a cheerleader for everyone in my life and those I do not know because I really do want us all to win! But gone are the days where I am pouring into everyone and everything else without pouring into myself. I also no longer feel guilty when I respectfully decline an invitation to different activities or events (although there have been very few because we are still in a pandemic). Sometimes I need to just be at home resting while my cup fills back up.

My health has now become a priority and I consistently workout four to five days a week while also eating healthier than ever before. I have rediscovered how much I love Art in all forms and had the audacity to go on a couple of dates by myself. My favorite occurred on a cloudy day in 2021. I grabbed a book and went to the Urban Hang Suite for lunch (one of my favorites!) and then I went to the Virginia Museum of Fine Arts to walk around and look at the many exhibits. I was so relaxed and enjoyed my own company.

You see, I do not know how much longer I have to live on this earth, but the lessons learned during this pandemic have been essential to my spiritual, mental, emotional, and physical health. I am one of the ones who will declare that I am NOT going back to normal because that just does not work for me anymore. I am about to start my fourth decade of life and I have never felt freer.

Is my life still busy? Yes, but only because I have balanced it with pouring into myself while giving to others. It is a different type of exhaustion, an exciting one even. I am going after dreams that I once had - writing being one of them - and I have started an HR consulting business. I am doing all of this scared most days, but I keep pressing forward. I only have one life to live and I choose to go after everything the devil thought he stole from me!

Tynesha Marie, formally known as Tynesha O'Quinn, was born and raised in Buffalo, NY (GO BILLS!). She currently lives in Raleigh, NC with her husband, Travis, and their two children, Sarai and Daniel. Tynesha currently works as a Human Resources professional, but she is exploring entrepreneurial opportunities with her own HR Consulting business – FINE HR Consulting – Operating in excellence, providing white-glove service!

Faith, family, and community are the most important things to Tynesha. If she isn't spending time with loved ones or volunteering, she can be found reading a book or writing, both of which are her first loves. Tynesha is currently working on several writing projects including a children's book, her memoir, and an HR-related book.

Learn more about Tynesha online at www.finehrconsulting.com or on LinkedIn as Tynesha O'Quinn.

Acknowledgements

Sadeqa Johnson
12th Street Press
www.sadeqajohnson.net
Facebook: @sadeqajohnson
Instagram: @SadeqaSays
LinkedIn: sadeqajohnson

Monique Morton
https://www.linkedin.com/in/monique-morton-47102116a/

Chrishawn Finister
DFW Assessment
https://dfwassessment.com
LinkedIn.com/ChrishawnFinister

Bouncing Back from Life's Setbacks like a B.O.S.S.

Dr. Tabatha M. W. Spurlock

"For I know the plans I have for you," declares the Lord, "plans to prosper you and not to harm you, plans to give you hope and a future." Jeremiah 29:11

It was 2009 and my husband and I were three years into our marriage and living in our first home built from the ground up. I frequently hosted Sunday football gatherings with friends, birthday and anniversary outings with other couples, and we traveled two to three times a year with either friends or family. I was a teacher working for an alternative program in our local school district and my husband was an auditor. While we weren't where we ultimately wanted to be career-wise, we were on track to get there for our family.

Life was good until one day there was a shift. We were having a conversation and my husband felt like one of us needed a six-figure income to advance to our next level. We made beyond six-figures collectively but not individually. Neither of us honestly remembers how and why he chose that amount, but that became the goal. My husband, who only had a bachelor's degree by choice, quickly declined the opportunity to go back to school for a master's degree. Neither of us were in a position to move up in our careers without additional certifications, licensures or degrees. While I had a business degree with a concentration in small business and entrepreneurship, I didn't have any solid examples to follow post-graduation. I always wanted to be a business owner and entrepreneur, but even with my degree I was stuck on how to make it happen.

After exploring our limited options, I decided to take one for the team and return to school for the last time. I would spend the next four years pursuing a doctorate degree that would ultimately cost just as much as we were seeking annually in income. Why would I do that? In hindsight, it made sense at the time and I'm glad I know otherwise now. But that's all we knew then and I was willing to do whatever I could to help elevate and support our family.

I was accepted into a Doctor of Education program with a concentration in Leadership and Technology at the University of Phoenix. I opted for an online program, although at a higher cost, to afford me a work/life balance. Attending online classes allowed me to continue working my full-time job and to be home in the evenings with my family. I was required to successfully pass over 60 credit hours of courses, attend four residencies away from home, write and defend a dissertation to fulfill graduation requirements. It was an extremely demanding program that required a high level of time management skills and perseverance. I accepted the challenge!

I did my best not to neglect my family or my financial obligations for our household. I had to get creative with my time daily. Instead of socializing with colleagues on my lunch breaks, I was at my desk reading articles and writing. During the week, I was in my home office most nights between 11:00 PM and 3:00 AM completing assignments only to be up by 6:30 AM to get ready for work. On the weekends, I was a traveling scholar. I recall one Saturday night where I had my laptop with me at the bowling alley to meet a deadline for an assignment. The pressure of not hanging with our friends, like we did prior to the program, was heavy. Honestly, I don't know how I held it together for so long...BUT GOD!

The finish line was in sight! I had attended Year 1 and 2 residencies and was on track to finish this four-year program on time. I had two of the best accountability partners that I connected with during Year 1. We were constantly encouraging and supporting one another. And as before, life was about to happen again. On December 13, 2010, I went to the doctor for an annual checkup only to be told that I was PREGNANT with my first and only child. Talk about an influx of emotions. I did not expect to hear that news in that season of life, but my husband and I were both happy about it.

Ready or not, it was time to level up! We were still pursuing the six-figure lifestyle, but another shift was pending. We decided to build our second home to accommodate our family's growth and this new home would be our forever home. Our beautiful daughter, Kennedi Alyse, was born on my late grandmother's birthday, August 26th. I thought we were fine until one day my husband shared with me that he felt his financial ends were no longer meeting.

We were parents of a newborn in a larger home and obviously our household expenses had increased. We didn't have support from family to help with our daughter when it was time for me to return to work. However, I found the best neighborhood daycare facility that became our daughter's second home for us working parents. They loved her and treated her like she was their own. We never had to worry about our child while she was enrolled at The Village Learning Center. All of the staff and teachers quickly became our extended family.

I honestly thought we were fine because we capitalized on a home with an additional 1,000 square feet for a mere $400 per month more than the monthly mortgage on our first house due to the housing market crash in 2011. It was a no brainer and win-win for me! By this time, I had received a promotion at work so I could contribute more to the monthly budget. However, my husband didn't feel the same on his end.

I continued to push through my coursework like a champion. I had a 4.0 grade point average and I was determined to finish strong. One more residency and a dissertation to go and smooth sailing from here…so I thought! I arrived at Year 3 residency in Arlington, Virginia - less than two hours from home. I got a random phone call from my best friend saying "Hey, I thought you were away this weekend but I'm at your house. Your husband invited a bunch of us over for a business presentation." And that was the beginning of a consecutive eight-year roller coaster ride with our home-based business. It also was the reason I soon became what's known as ABD (all but dissertation) shortly after I left Year 3 residency.

Instead of discussing with me how "we" would make our ends meet, my husband independently decided to pursue an entrepreneurial venture with a former college friend. This friend was making six-figures from home and my husband got excited. He thought my plan, our agreed upon plan, wasn't happening fast enough and he needed an immediate fix to our financial problems. Can you imagine my devastation? How dare he? How could he? I was only a year, two max, from completing a doctoral program that I got roped into because of his aspirations for our family. Oh, did I mention that my financial aid was running low and I would soon have to pay for my final courses out of pocket?

It was time for the superwoman cape to come off. I couldn't continue to meet my academic deadlines with an infant while feeling like a single parent due to the self-imposed demands of the business by my husband. He was building the business at a fast pace. While it was admirable, it was taxing on me physically, mentally and emotionally. Overnight, I had to check out of my own goals and dreams for our family because he found a quick replacement. For the next two years, our home-based business was earning at least $50,000 annually. Oh, did I mention that my husband got fired from his good city government job one month after he began this business venture? At this point, the math really wasn't mathing for me. He was making less than he was at his full-time job and going further into debt. It was time for an executive decision.

I agreed to put my degree on hold for an entire year to support my husband in any capacity needed. Primarily, I cared for the children (our daughter and my bonus child) while holding down a full-time job and assisting with the business on a part-time basis. I allowed him the freedom and flexibility to get us to the six-figure mark. There was also the potential of earning up to $30,000 in bonus money. The bonus was motivating for me, especially since I needed at least $10-15,000 to finish the doctoral program. I told my husband let's do it. I even created a word wall and vision board to keep us motivated and on track. I'm pleased to say that we met the goal of becoming $100,000 income earners within one year. We also were in good standing to receive the bonus, but was later told that we didn't meet the requirements. Apparently, the rules changed once the contest started. I was devastated!

No degree, no bonus money, and now my husband's ego was out of control. How did I allow myself to be in this situation? He didn't honor his promise to return the support after achieving the six-figure goal for me to finish my degree and it made me feel stuck. I didn't even recognize myself or my life at that moment. I thought we were building generational wealth for our family only to realize my husband was living his best entrepreneurial life at the expense of his wife and family. What seemed like a great opportunity began to feel like a nightmare. In my heart and mind, I was submitting to my husband and gave him full reign to guide us into financial security and that next level lifestyle. The money was being made, yet the household wasn't seeing it. Within three years, our forever home was headed into foreclosure and both of our luxury vehicles repossessed.

Enough was enough! It was time to bounce back from life's setbacks like a boss. Here's how I did it and how you can too:

B: Break away from distractions - Distance yourself from any and every one feeding negative energy and/or words into your spirit. Realize that some situations and relationships require boundaries.

O: Own your decisions - Stay true to your thoughts and feelings without caving into the pressures of others'. You won't always make others happy so learn how to say NO and mean it.

S: Stop asking for permission trying to please others and take back your power - Live your life unapologetically!

S: Show up for yourself - Finish that degree…did! Buy the car…did! Take the trip…did! Build the business and write the book…did and went best-seller!

While I loved my husband dearly and still do, life had become overwhelming. I had to regain control of my life after realizing I was losing myself. I had to pick myself up by my own bootstraps because no one was coming to save me...not even my husband. For once in my life, I didn't have the answers, yet I had to figure them out. I was in survival mode and the perceived support by the general public from what they saw on social media wasn't my reality. I was fighting battles left and right with my head barely above water. In the end, I chose peace. It's easy to say what you will and won't deal with in life until you're in a position to deal with said things. I chose to fight through the hurt, pain, betrayal, and disrespect one day at a time still honoring the vows I took before God with dignity and self-respect.

Dr. Tabatha Spurlock is a mother, entrepreneur, 2X best-selling author, philanthropist, highly energetic motivational speaker, educator and wife for over 15 years. She also volunteers with several community organizations and enjoys serving as a mentor and board member for a nonprofit organization called MEGA Mentors. This leader has a true servant's heart and desire to help uplift, motivate, and inspire others.

Over the years, she's had several life experiences that led her to the superwoman role. Those experiences included being strong and resilient despite financial losses, failed relationships, and two traumatic accidents. As she continues to navigate life, she understands that there are times when the cape must be put on the shelf. With her "Like a B.O.S.S." method, she has learned how to bounce back from life's setbacks with ease.

Learn more about Dr. Tabatha Spurlock online at www.empower1inspiremany.com or follow her on Instagram at @empower1inspiremany.

… Dr. Tabatha Spurlock

Acknowledgements

Vicki Neilson

Dr. Gwyn Moses
Author
www.drgwynrcmoses.com
Facebook: @authorgwynrcmoses

Anissa Cushionberry
Facebook: @anissacushionberry
Instagram: @bayouprincess79

Evelyn Haye-Primus
Creative Expressions & Gifts
www.creativeexpressionsandgifts.com
https://www.facebook.com/creativeexpressionsandgifts
Instagram:@Creativeexpressionsandgifts
https://www.linkedin.com/company/creative-expressions-&-gifts

Dr. Lita Jackson
Laine DiCarlo
www.lainedicarlo.com
Facebook: @LaineDicarloBeauty
Instagram: @lainedicarlobeauty

Phynise Boisseau- Williams
Facebook: Phynise Boisseau- Williams
Instagram: @Niseyb1

Karmelle Hendrick-Marshall
HiSiDiTi Catering
Facebook: @HiSiDiTiCatering
Instagram: @HiSiDiTiCatering

Adina Porter
Sunshine Body Care LLC
www.sunshinebodycare.net
Facebook: @sunshinebodycarellc
Instagram: @sunshinebodycare

Tiffany Martin
Martin&Co Events
Eventsbymartinandco.as.me
Instagram: @Eventsbymartinandco

Charlene Bates

Pamela Spratley
The Enough Foundation
Facebook: @theenoughfoundationrva
Instagram: @theenoughfoundationrva

Samantha Mitchell
ST. Mitchell LLC
www.confidencemba.com
Facebook: Samantha Mitchell
Instagram:@Sam2transform
https://www.linkedin.com/in/samantha-t-mitchell-20486896

Vernice Cooper
Vacate Victimville
www.vacatevictimville.net
Facebook: @vacatevictimville
Instagram: @vacatevictimville
LinkedIn: Vernice Cooper

Tynesha Ellis
Sunshineandkeys LLC
Facebook: @sunshineandkeys
Instagram: @sunshineandkeys

Dorian Ridley-Curtis

Dr. Tabatha Spurlock
No More Running
www.empower1inspiremany.com
Instagram: @n0morerunning

The Wearing Of The Cape
Shania Taylor

The wearing of the cape begins so early on in life and oftentimes, it just goes unnoticed. As a little girl, around age eight or so, I can remember wanting the Superwoman t-shirt and panty set. I believe they were called underoos. Half of the girls in my class had them and I just couldn't wait to get mine. Once I received it, I wore them nearly every day. That S on that shirt had little meaning other than Superwoman, the beautiful Lynda Carter, who wore the S on her chest along with her cape on a mission to save the world. A fictional character she was - or was she? At such a tender age, we were learning as we grew. We were also made to do as we were told by the adults in our lives. Those little responsibilities like taking out trash, cleaning the kitchen, and tidying our room - which seemed so big when we were forced to do so - molded us. Even weekend trips to my grandmother's home came with responsibilities and chores of some kind. For some, we sustained that same mentality as we grew into adulthood. I'm sure some will agree that we are always aiming to please others.

Having children early in life, I hardly had time to myself. By age 19, I had already had two children and was raising them as a single parent. Even though parenting came naturally for me due to always being in caretaker mode in my youth, it still came with its challenges. I often prayed for a decent loving man - not just for me, but for my girls as well. He had to be as fit for them as he was for me. Psalm 27:14 states, "Wait on the Lord: be of good courage. And he shall strengthen thine heart." I must admit, I didn't understand the Bible much growing up, but there was something powerful about that phrase "Wait on the Lord."

Soon I started dating Gerard. He was everything I wanted and needed in a spouse. He wasn't just perfect for me, but for my two girls as well. We had so much in common and his family was fond of me and mine was of him. Gerard doted on the girls and me. Soon, we were residing together and it wasn't long before we started talking of growing our family. We had baby girl number three and I was at the happiest moment in my life. Even with the endless cooking and cleaning, turning back the sheets later and later, I wouldn't have traded it for anything in the world. Not to say that being in a relationship and living together was peaches and cream; we had our little arguments from time to time. I realized later on in life that they were foolish.

I feel like I took him for granted believing that he would always be here. Then Boom! The saddest day of my life arrived, November 18th. It started out as what I thought would be a normal day, but I kept having bouts of unexplained sadness. The children were going with my sister for the night as Gerard and I were set to attend a party with some friends of ours. We laughed and talked as we got ready for our night out. Then out of the blue, the conversation turned cold. Gerard started talking about death and where he wanted to be buried if something were to ever happen to him. He said he wanted to be buried with his mother. Even though I didn't understand, I assured him that I would carry out his wishes. He told me he loved me and to always keep my head up and to be strong for our girls. That feeling of sadness returned as I watched the seriousness in his face. My sister came for the girls and Gerard, my little brother and I headed for the party. In the car, Gerard barely spoke another word as the radio played his favorite song "Ain't No Sunshine When She's Gone." It played over and over. We arrived at the party and mingled around with friends before tragedy struck. A confrontation broke out and with me standing short of arm's length of my lover, POW! POW! POW! I watched

The Wearing of the Cape

as Gerard was shot in the head by an individual. Blood splattered on my face and covered my off-white blouse that I was wearing. All I could do was scream as his lifeless body hit the floor. My world stopped. I laid on the floor beside him for a moment until the gunfire ceased. I remember begging him please not to leave me, that the girls and I needed him. He just laid motionless as blood bubbled from his nose. I tried administering CPR until I was removed from the scene, but not before hearing the officer tell my brother that Gerard was gone. My whole world had come to an end. The man I loved, the father of my children, was gone.

What did I do wrong? Where was my strength? Why wasn't it enough to save him? The S on my chest was gone and my days became dull. I couldn't see light because the darkness always overcame me. It was then I felt the pain. My heart was really hurting physically. It was then I fully understood what it means to die of a broken heart. Love is an action word but so is pain and I didn't know how much more I could take. Depression swarmed me so badly that my hair started falling out. I had lost over 20 pounds and finally was admitted to the hospital where I stayed for a little over a week. Mind you, that hospital staff never addressed the trauma behind the tragedy. Why wasn't the severity of my pain addressed? I was traumatized even when I tried to sleep. I would replay that tragic night in my dreams and it kept haunting me. But while at the hospital, I knew I had to get back home to my children. I had to pick up my cape and get back to raising them amongst other duties.

When I made it back home, the closing of the window blinds began. My room was dark day and night. I didn't want to see the day and was glad when night fell. I was drowning before my loved ones but knew how to hide it. I would push away anyone who tried to love or befriend me. All I wanted to do was drown. I functioned and smiled throughout the day, babysitting amongst other things for others, and sank during the night. I really didn't know how to say NO! even though I was not mentally well myself. My house always stayed full of other people's children and problems. Meanwhile, I was literally under water. Then one night after the tears, I took comfort in something my mom once told me. Whenever I had sleepless nights, or days, mind racing with no comfort in sight, I sought God, Allah as she called him. For God's promise is He will never leave me nor forsake me. That gave me the extra boost to continue on with life. But what it didn't give me was the ability to seek my needs before others.

You know a stove has four burners, two in the front and two in the back. Well let's say I was the back burner. My needs came second to everyone else's needs. I had to learn how to prioritize. In doing so, I set myself on a schedule and didn't allow anyone's needs before it. Second, I had to change my mindset. Just because money was in my account didn't mean it was in my budget to give. I had to learn not to give to others so freely - whether it was my time or funds. But why did my "no" make me feel so guilty? Like not giving of myself is a crime. Third, I got tired of watching others' success stories unfold before my face while my dreams were all put on hold. I know that goals are better achieved once written, so I started writing them down and checking them off as I achieved them. I would even go as far as treating myself to something nice for goals accomplished. Few things down, more to go.

Years passed and I completed my family with four girls and one boy - half the baseball team, as some would say. After raising all five of them and working 9-5 as a CNA, I came home still in caretaker mode just when my life was to begin as my children were growing into adults. I spent ten more years caring for an ailing family member in my home. Thankfully, I can say after his death, I have no regrets. But, there was my dream of becoming an author on hold once again. I was back burning myself once more for others' needs. Or was I drowning in excuses? EXCUSES! Then one night while sleeping, I heard a voice say, "Be Still." I couldn't tell if I was awake or really dreaming, but I fell to my knees in prayer that next morning asking God to please grant me the strength to accomplish all things that I set forth to do. But first I felt I had to be obedient to His word because I was always pleasing man but I knew I needed to be pleasing Him. I knew that He would never leave me nor forsake me. I had to let go and let God!

In Him, I gained my strength. I began to put everyone's needs on the back burner and I became that front aisle. I learned to say no, no, no and I began to live again. I gained back enough trust in mankind to allow a few people next to me, as I lost so much trust in death. I was allowing myself to live outside of the fence I had built around me. Words of advice when overcoming trauma: Seek help. Don't feel ashamed as I did because I felt it made me appear fragile. Don't shelter yourself away from those who love you. There will be dark days but you must allow light. In the same token, don't allow others to bombard your healing. Allowing oneself peace in troubled times is detrimental and part of the healing process. Moreover, learning to step back and allow others to step in sometimes allowed for self-care for me. As a caretaker, we frequently take care of others and abort ourselves. Lastly, what we do for others should come with limits because a lack of boundaries could be like an egg with no shell. Learning to love me more gave me the understanding that it was okay to walk to the door hook and hang up the cape. I can be just as strong with a lowercase s as I was with a capitalized S.

Shania Princess Taylor is the author of Who Silenced The Well. She has a passion for writing and does so through fearless characters that she brings to life through her novels. Shania praises her love for reading as a child for her accomplishments of today. In her spare time, she still enjoys reading novels by others. Look out for more phenomenal reads in the coming future from Shania.

Stay in touch with Shania via email at Princessshania72@icloud.com.

Acknowledgements

Barbara Muhammad

Tyrone Cloyd, Jr.

Tyren Cloyd

James Dixon

Rakita Lewis

Rakia Taylor

Tynetta Thomas

Brenda Grooms

Takiya Taylor
NLSAW Counseling
www.nlsawcounseling.com
Facebook: @Nlsaw

No Longer Boxed In
Marcella Tazewell

People underestimate their capacity for change. There is never a right time to do a difficult thing.
— Archer John Porter Martin

In a way, we all love the idea of being a Superwoman until we realize this role is costing me too much. For many years, I was a Superwoman - a wife, mom, daughter, church member, and employee. I balanced all of these roles all while carrying the burdens of disappointment, the mindset of let's fix what's wrong (in marriage, family, and self), and fulfilling the "yes" in church, parenthood, and my place of employment. If you're exhausted after reading that then imagine how this Superwoman felt for several years. You may even be thinking – gosh, this sounds like me! If you can relate, then keep reading and let me help you a little.

If truth be told, my heart was always in the right place, but I did not have the capacity to withstand it all effectively. I was a Superwoman on many days operating out of fear, lack and the perspective of others. With all that being said, I want to share with you the when, the why, the resolution and most importantly, the freedom of my life change.

The When
When the divorce happened, I was so shocked. I honestly had no words and felt so low and shameful even though not many people knew what I was struggling with. I realized that I could not be a Superwoman when my emotional and mental

health became a concern for me. It was so concerning that I would have to remind myself that I was not in the battles that I faced alone. Many times I felt like I could only rely on God! Now, don't get super spiritual on me and say God should have been more than enough because we all reach a time when we are like, "God, is this all the help You got for me??!!" Like some women, my issues with life did not shine brighter than my smile or like the amazing words I could speak. However, the more my marriage began to suffer, the more I thought I could not do this (tuff persona) anymore. I could not try to fix my problems and his problems. I could not say "yes" to the church when I felt hurt by some of the actions of the people. I no longer could fake the smile and hide the pain. No matter what I said to fight for unity in my marriage or the self-changes I made, nothing seemed to completely work because it needed two willing people to be on one accord in the journey. When I knew for sure my Superwoman abilities were landing below half, I also had to remember that both people were human and flawed.

During the separation process, I questioned so much around me! I questioned my upbringing, myself (strengths and weaknesses), my relationship with God and the church, my parenting, and the foundation on which my marriage was built upon. About six months into my experience, I began to look and worry more about myself after a few emotional breakdowns. I would black out and not be able to see my way clearly. I realized my foundation of so many things had been built off what was not sustainable. This portion may give insight to my marriage at the time, but it was more about me than anything. It was about My Why! It was about My Perspective! It was about what I was Holding On To! It was about My Fear!

The Why

You want to know why I took off the Superwoman cape? I took it off because I was hurting myself more than helping myself. The YES was a mess at times. I wasn't free or proud of what my life had become. At times, I was not even proud of who I had become. I was inwardly scared, emotionally traumatized, suffering from childhood trauma and hiding behind the cross, as the older saints would say. Superwoman did not help me be a better person, wife or mother which, during this time, were the roles I took great pride in. As a church member, daughter and worker - yes, I could be accounted for and meet the need - but often I was in autopilot mode. I wasn't fully engaged because the best parts of me had been in the sacrifices I chose to make as a wife and mom. I was masked and covered up! It is safe to say I was always in character.

The Superwoman cape came off because I could no longer say YES to pleasing others with the image of perfection. I could no longer say YES to being fearful of what could be if I stopped trying to fix everything. It had to come off because my YES was hurting me! Yes to love with conditions from multiple areas of my life just didn't work anymore. What about taking the cape off so my kids could see the real me versus the mom that was always on the go, tired, smiling, but not always emotionally available? I took the cape off even when it came to being the close to perfect daughter. I had to because my upbringing, just like many of ours, planted seeds in me as a young child that did not always produce healthy results. I could no longer say yes to what my parents wanted to see. This NO became very personal to me. It was me or my life!! I didn't want to imagine my life any longer as anything less than happy and free! I desired balance for myself and my children. I wanted to see rebirth by any means. In the beginning, I struggled with the NO, but then it got good to me!

The Resolution
I'm a church girl and a lover of Jesus Christ with all my heart and soul. I was raised in church and have seen so many people triumph over many things. My parents were a starting example. So, my resolution was simple. For me, it was to get so real with God that He just might say, "Girl, I'm tired of you!" I began to evaluate myself more than my significant other. At times, it may have not seemed that way, but truth be told, I was on a mission to carve off all the pieces of me that I could in order to see change. I began to say I want to live a happy life during sad or mad moments and not the other way around. I began to pray more for me and the things I saw in myself that may have been hidden from others. I began to feed my mind positivity. I talked to very close friends that had proper perspective and not just the ones who said "yes" to everything. I stood tall in my truth no matter what it was. I walked in environments that I knew gossiped about me or mishandled me. I needed to feel some of what I feared because I knew it would strengthen me. I had no real reason to be ashamed because I always did my best. The flipside is I'm not perfect so I apologized for anything I could think of concerning my marriage at the time and even to my children just to get it off of me. I became more aware of my triggers. I began to say NO more.

I said NO with the intentions of setting healthy boundaries, healing, and becoming more focused on what would produce goodness in my life. I began to go against some of what was expected of me! I began to look fear, insecurities, guilt, shame, religion, and trauma in the face. I walked with my head held high because I knew that my results would say wholeness very soon. Truth be told, the walk-through released some things that I held dear such as the marriage and the church I was attending at the time. Both served a purpose in my life and neither I regret but I had to learn to let go of them both. I didn't let go because I was perfect or to place blame, but to be free because maybe it was time. The walk-through/resolution also placed many people around me that put me in uncomfortable situations, but the cape still had to come off because I had no real power with it on. The real Superwoman showed up and understood her strength came from within! Her strength could not be measured by the show but by the courage to stand tall, unmasked, unashamed and willing to grow as she plucked up things from the root of her heart.

I hope as you read this you understand that the failing marriage was a trigger, not because perfection was required, but because it was the biggest security blanket I had created. It was made from so much love, but it wasn't very secure due to the mindsets it was built on. It was a safety net for two people who had experienced much as individuals, but much as a couple. However, the root cause was a mindset that was built off Superwoman tendencies even from childhood for me. I was an only child and I was used to solving and rationalizing things on my own. I protected myself in some situations that left me feeling unprotected. At times, I had only one present parent and that caused me issues in so many ways emotionally. The walk-through helped me realize that my NO was healing me from my past to my present. No longer could I reserve the right to protect the image when I deserved the right to pure resolution. The resolution required me to be brave!

The Freedom
Without the Superwoman cape I found Freedom, Joy, and Myself Again. One part of my life may have triggered the need to come out of Superwoman status, but so many elements of my life contributed to the unhealthy version of

why I felt the need to play the role in an unhealthy way. The freedom looks like discovering me on the daily without the pressed opinions of others. It has given me the liberty to explore so many new things such as hair, style, travel and even my relationship with God. I'm free in my heart and mind. This has been so liberating because I don't have to guard it so closely. I'm not constantly in "what if" mode. I've learned to love parts of me that at one time I did not like. I see me for me! This freedom has allowed me to embrace my children in a healthier way such as tending to their emotional and mental well-being. It has allowed me to be more open with them and I've found parenting a joy versus a task. The NO as Superwoman has allowed me to say YES to healing and an abundant life. I have started a life coaching business called Heart Social because I realized we all experience things in life that affect us at any stage in life but the key is to be open and aware enough to desire change. Then we must be bold and courageous enough to do the work. Your future is waiting on your healing because your healing will allow you to make better decisions for what is to come in life.

So, say No to being Superwoman and say YES to being YOU. You're enough and you don't have to save the world to prove it.

Marcella Tazewell is the owner of Heart Social, a Life Coaching company. Heart Social helps Marcella reach people in a casual, yet heart felt way. Marcella strives to empower, uplift, and help cultivate the very part of you that you want to see exhale. Moreover, she helps you to see life from another perspective in which healing and growth can take place. Being a mother to two beautiful and amazing children is the thing that brings Marcella's heart and life the most joy.

So much of who she has become and what she does is because she knows they are watching. Marcella is a believer of Jesus Christ and believes that He has called us to live a life of abundance. She is also a daughter - which keeps her humble -and a walking testimony of life's ups, downs, and victories.

Learn more about Marcella online:
Instagram: @heart_social
Facebook: Heart Social
Website: heart-social.square.site/

Acknowledgements

Ashley Simpson
Fancy Pants
Facebook: @ashleysimpson and @fancypants
Instagram: @plus_size_barb and @thee_red_lip

Cekeiya Cook

Sherry Gordon

Mautricia Young
Facebook: @Triciyoung

Sophia McEachin
Instagram:@luvlyzeta
linkedin.com/in/sophia-mceachin-cic-cisr-api-ais-ains-aic-900538144

Denise Wilkerson

Jennifer Clayton
Dreamz Restaurant and Banquet Hall
Facebook: Jennifer Clayton
Instagram: @thareal_jlo

Deandra Fletcher

Antonio & Michelle Tazewell

Juankneca Wilson

Conclusion

Congratulations! You made it to the end of this book which likely means the stories of the women resonated with you and you too are serious about taking back your power. Setting boundaries is not always easy, especially when you're naturally a nurturer and always want to lend a helping hand. Saying no to others just to say yes to yourself may even seem selfish to some. But always remember, self-care is not selfish; it's necessary. Though it may take some time, those who love and depend on you will thank you in the long run for prioritizing yourself because you'll be even better equipped to serve them. And frankly, you don't have to be a Superwoman to do that. You can just be you!

Made in the USA
Columbia, SC
31 May 2024